The Mother Nature Guidebook

The

MOTHER NATURE GUIDEBOOK

Exploring the journey of motherhood

Ági Berecz, Jana Lemke,
Lara Kastelic, Looby Macnamara,
Sara Galeotti and Valentina Cifarelli

The Mother Nature Guidebook: Exploring the Journey of Motherhood
Authors: Ági Berecz, Jana Lemke, Lara Kastelic, Looby Macnamara, Sara Galeotti and Valentina Cifarelli, with contributions from Doreen Hertrampf and Lily Rose Sequoia.

Published by Greyhound Self-Publishing, 2020

Printed and bound by Aspect Design
89 Newtown Road, Malvern, Worcs. WR14 1PD
United Kingdom
Tel: 01684 561567
E-mail: allan@aspect-design.net
Website: www.aspect-design.net

All Rights Reserved.

This guidebook was written and produced during the Mother Nature project, funded by the Erasmus+ programme of the European Union.

Drawings and cover: Eszter Laszlo

Graphic design: Sara Galeotti

Copyright © 2020, Mother Nature Project

All rights reserved.

You may not sell, alter or further reproduce or distribute any part of this book to any other person without the permission of the authors. If the material is provided to you in electronic format you may download or print from it for your own use. You may not download or make a further copy for any other purpose.

A copy of this book has been deposited with the British Library Board

ISBN 978-1-909219-64-9

This book is for the first teachers, creators, sustainers, nurturers.

It is for Mothers.

Mothers of children of all ages, mothers of all races, all backgrounds, from all cultures, and mothers without children.

We are mothers to children we may have lost, or to babies who never made it earth-side.

There are many ways to become a mother. We may be mothers to big ideas, projects, communities and to other people's children.

Mothering is a manifestation of our creative energy.

'Helping women become conscious mothers. This is perhaps the greatest way we can help bring peace to this world.'
Gurmukh Kaur Khalsa

'Not only does the mother give birth to her child, through the child the mother herself is born.'
Gertrud von Le Fort

CONTENTS

THE MOTHER NATURE COMMUNITY — XIII
THIS GUIDEBOOK — XIV
THE MOTHER NATURE TOOLS — XV
OUR RESPONSIBILITY — XV
ACKNOWLEDGEMENT AND GRATITUDE — XVI
DISCLAIMER — XVI
THE MOTHER NATURE PRINCIPLES AND FAMILIES — XVII

THE JOURNEY — 1
LISTEN TO THE CALL — 2
CROSS THE THRESHOLD — 4
BEFRIEND YOUR DRAGONS — 6
BE WITH THE DARKNESS — 8
FIND YOUR ELIXIR — 10
MAKE PEACE WITH YOUR SHADOW — 12
COME INTO ALIGNMENT — 14

REFRAME CHALLENGES — 17
FACE DEEP PATTERNS — 18
RELAX INTO THE UNKNOWN — 20
LOVE YOUR NEW BODY — 22
DARE TO SAY NO — 24
IT'S GOOD TO DO NOTHING — 26
YOU ARE YOUR OWN ANCHOR — 28
YOU ARE GOOD ENOUGH — 30

TRANSFORM — 33

- CONNECT WITH YOUR ROOTS AND ANCESTORS — 34
- CREATE SOMETHING — 36
- YOU ARE A LEADER — 38
- LET GO — 40
- BIRTHING IS YOUR INITIATION — 42
- OPEN TO EMERGENCE — 44
- MEET THE GODDESS — 46

EMPOWER — 49

- LISTEN — 50
- PRACTICE SELF-CARE WITH YOUR CHILD — 52
- GIVE GRATITUDE — 54
- ASK FOR HELP AND BE PROACTIVE — 56
- NOURISH COMMUNITY — 58
- TRUST YOUR INTUITION — 60
- DESIGN YOUR LIFE PATH — 62

NOURISH YOUR GIFTS — 65

- FIND YOUR STRENGTH — 66
- MOTHERHOOD IS JOY — 68
- YOUR GIFT IS EFFECTIVENESS — 70
- EMBRACE YOUR VULNER-ABILITY — 72
- BECOME SELF-AWARE — 74
- RECEIVE THE GIFT OF PATIENCE — 76
- EMBRACE YOUR FEMININE POWER — 78

CONNECT WITH NATURE   81
    GET OUT, GET WILD!   82
    YOU ARE NATURE   84
    YOUR CHILD IS YOUR NATURE MENTOR   86
    CARE FOR EARTH   88
    GROUND YOURSELF   90
    CONNECT WITH THE PLANT WORLD   92
    ALIGN WITH NATURAL PATTERNS AND CYCLES   94

MOTHER NATURE CIRCLES GUIDE   97
    ABOUT MOTHER NATURE CIRCLES   98
    FLOW OF THE CIRCLE MEETINGS   99

ABOUT THE AUTHORS   105

ORGANISATIONS   111

ENDNOTES   117

THE MOTHER NATURE COMMUNITY

MOTHER NATURE is a community of mothers, women and people supporting mothers. We are committed to creating a worldwide movement of sisterhood, bringing awareness to the personal transformation journey of mothers.

We understand motherhood as a time of personal growth and realignment of our life path. Connecting with nature and other mothers can be a source of comfort and support during this pivotal period. At MOTHER NATURE we are advocates of conscious motherhood, without promoting any particular parenting style.

The original framework for our cooperation was a European learning partnership project running from November 2017 until January 2020. The partnership started with the strong commitment, purpose and vision of twelve women and one man: Ági Berecz, Anita Šerjak Koci, Doreen Hertrampf, Elena Salvucci, Emese Dömösi, Eszter László, Jana Lemke, Lara Kastelic, Liza Baranyai, Looby Macnamara, Roberto Cardinale, Sara Galeotti and Valentina Cifarelli, from Hungary, Germany, Italy, Slovenia and the United Kingdom.

Our aim is to create supportive communities of mothers and equip them with tools to learn about their journeys as mothers. One of these tools, the MOTHER NATURE Journey Course offers women a space to gather, learn and share about their journey of becoming mothers. Courses are based on six face-to-face meetings, and are run by group leaders trained with our facilitator's training. We launched our MOTHER NATURE Journey Courses in autumn 2019 in Hungary, Germany, Italy, Slovenia and the UK.

THIS GUIDEBOOK

Our forty-two principles in this guidebook are daily affirmations that help us to be present and aware of our journey of motherhood. They are not the recommendations of experts, nor scientific or religious truths, they come from our life experience as mothers. They are elixirs, a-ha moments, distillations of our joys, struggles, challenges and learnings from our lives as mothers.

In June 2018 in Terény, Hungary at our first international MOTHER NATURE retreat, twenty-four mothers weaved together their everyday experiences and the initial version of the principles were born. Then we organised them into six 'families' and completed the text with reflective questions, activities and affirmations. Eszter meditated on all of the principles and married the principles with her enchanting images. Her paintings illustrate our MOTHER NATURE Card Deck. The cards and principles were used at our first European training for professionals in March 2018 in Mondaino, Italy. An international group of fifteen doulas, women circle leaders, midwives and counsellors added their insights to our ideas.

This guidebook and principles are manifestations of this co-creative work. They have evolved from our first hand experience as mothers, as well as our training in self development, mindfulness, nature connection and vision quests, Cultural Emergence and permaculture. Permaculture is a way of using nature as a guide for designing regenerative systems. Our aim is to design regenerative systems for us as mothers using these principles.

The principles can be used by mothers individually and in small self-organised MOTHER NATURE circles. If you are a counsellor or therapist working in one-to-one settings, you may use the principles in your work.

It is good to choose one of the principles at a time to work with, rather than try and read the whole guidebook from cover to cover. Ideally, if you have the Card Deck, you pick a card, or do one of the layouts suggested in the booklet accompanying the cards, and then come to the guidebook for further explanations, questions and activities.

Authors of the guidebook are Ági Berecz, Jana Lemke, Lara Kastelic, Looby Macnamara, Sara Galeotti and Valentina Cifarelli, with contributions from Doreen Hertrampf and Lily Rose Sequoia.

THE MOTHER NATURE RESOURCES AND TOOLS

The Mother Nature project has created this guidebook, a card deck, online community, mother's circles, Journey course and other events. The aim of all of these MOTHER NATURE resources is to empower mothers in their personal transformation, guide us to realign with our life path and foster our reconnection with Nature and the web of Life on Earth.

The MOTHER NATURE Card Deck is a great accompaniment to this guidebook. It contains these forty-two principles with the enchanting paintings of Eszter László. The cards are designed to help you live by these principles. They encourage you to understand the messages through your analogue right-brain and speak to your intuitive self. You can use the cards as daily inspiration and guidance, individually, in your group work and in one-to-one therapeutic settings.

Here, in chapter 7, you will find a guide for leading MOTHER NATURE circles. These circles are led by mothers, for mothers, and are based on our guidebook and card deck. They are a fantastic way to build a supportive community of mothers around you.

The MOTHER NATURE Journey course and other retreats and events are led by trained facilitators and support you to dive deeper into your own experience in an embodied, creative and relaxing way.

Please do join our online community of mothers to connect with other women and share stories, experiences and insights.

For more information of all of these resources and future projects please visit our website (www.mothernatureproject.org), and like our Facebook page (https://www.facebook.com/mothernatureproject).

OUR RESPONSIBILITY

Motherhood brings with it great responsibility. It calls on our ability to hold the unknown. Thinking about the future in the midst of the current ecological crisis can feel overwhelming. Anchoring our actions in honour of our children, our great, great, great, great grandchildren and all living beings who will walk this Earth after us, can help us to navigate this uncertainty.

We dedicate this work to the healing of our connection to Mother Earth and to honouring all life; our children's and future generations of all life forms.

ACKNOWLEDGEMENT AND GRATITUDE

We express our gratitude to Mother Nature, our Earth mother for carrying and sustaining us and filling our hearts and lives with beauty.

We are grateful for our mothers, grandmothers and ancestors for the lineage that has led us to the here and now, to find each other and dream together. We express our love and gratitude to our children for teaching us unconditional love: to Berta, Greta, Felix, Lenke, Livio, Mio, Remi, Shanti and Teya and to those on the way.

We are grateful and inspired by every woman walking the path of conscious motherhood and those supporting mothers. Especially for all those taking part in our training courses in Hungary, 2018 and in Italy, 2019 for their midwifery in birthing this publication. Heartfelt gratitude to the rest of the Mother Nature team, Anita Šerjak Koci, Doreen Hertrampf, Elena Salvucci, Emese Dömösi, Eszter László, Liza Baranyai and Roberto Cardinale, and to Katalin Orosz, Nelli Szénási, Zsuzsanna Egry, Lusi Alderslowe, Debora T. Stenta and Clara Scropetta, for their contribution, knowledge and inspiration. We greatly appreciate the support of our friends, Lily Rose Sequoia, Niamhue Robins, Ágoston Berecz, Gillian Hipp, Kate Rawson, Sarah Moonflower, Enrico Samorì and Anja Hausen in proofreading and editing the text.

We would like to thank our funders at the European Erasmus+ programme and everyone who believed that informal learning of mothers is an important area to invest in.

DISCLAIMER

MOTHER NATURE has an informal adult learning approach. Although, our tools may be used by trained counsellors and therapists to add value to the therapeutic process, please use them within your competence boundaries and use them with awareness and care.

Our tools are not meant to be solely used in therapeutic settings, and they cannot replace psychological or medical support.

THE MOTHER NATURE PRINCIPLES AND FAMILIES

The forty-two Mother Nature principles contained within this guidebook are also illustrated on the Mother Nature Card Deck. Each card of the deck represents a principle, which is an affirmation and guidance for our Mother's Journey. The principles are described here in more detail and with reflective questions and activities to further our understanding and connection with them. They have been derived from the collective wisdom of the Mother Nature group. The principles are placed within the following families:

- The Journey
- Reframe Challenges
- Transform
- Empower
- Nourish Your Gift
- Connect With Nature

These families relate to the aims of the Mother Nature project; supporting personal transformation, realigning with our life path and nature connection. Each family represents an aspect of the Mother's Journey, and they are all interlinked.

The Journey

The principles of the Journey family lead you through the Mother's Journey, the path of emotional maturation and personal development.

The principle **Listen to the call** invites you to leave behind your old maiden identity and bravely embark on the journey.

Cross the threshold represents becoming a mother as a rite of passage, a gateway into your new role of a mother.

This is a time of great upheaval. Trials in folktales are symbolised by dragons the hero meets along the journey. **Befriend your dragons** shows the usual 'dragons' of mothers and reminds you of the female path of taming them rather than fighting them: the path of seeking support, finding allies and creating a community of mothers.

Be with the darkness talks about an image repeated in ancient myths, the symbolic place of the 'belly of the whale', archetype of death and rebirth. A great crisis and capitulation, where you stop fighting, accept your changed situation as it is here and now. Rebirthing from the crisis of your changed

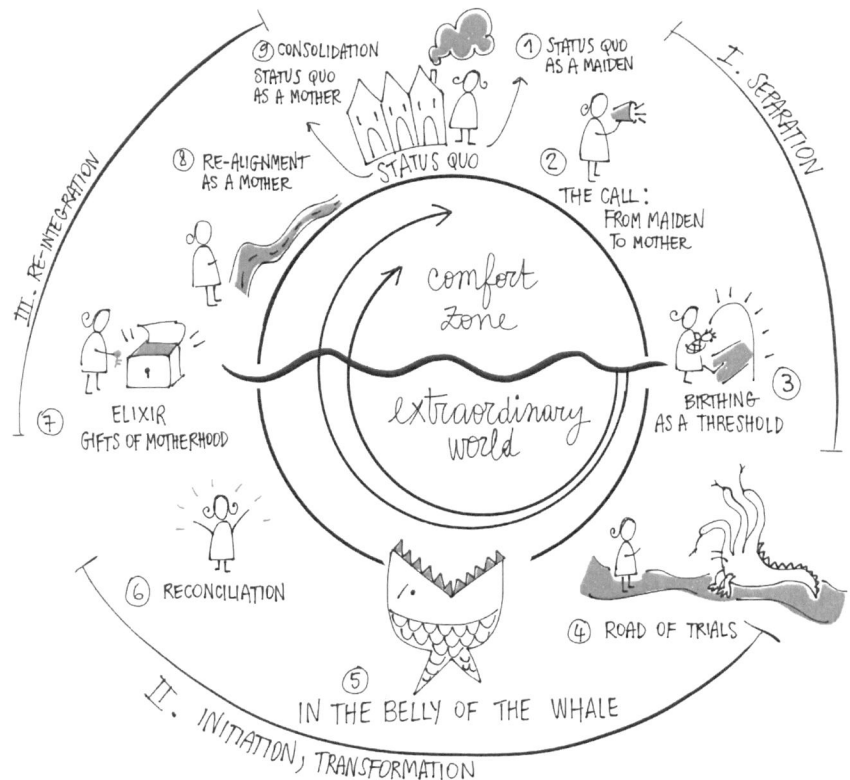

situation, you may find hardships have a meaning. They are there to teach you something and play an important role in your transformation as mother.

Find your elixir calls you to name and own these new parts of yourself; your gifts of motherhood.

Make peace with your shadow invites you to become aware of recurring patterns from family and childhood, themes that you can now face as an adult and shift.

Come into alignment is about finding harmony again, this time as a mother, fully transformed and aligned with the new stage of your life.

Reframe Challenges

The family of Reframe Challenges evolved from identifying the common challenges that mothers face. After identifying them we sought to find ways to overcome them. Often the challenges themselves cannot be resolved, but we can find ways to look at them differently. This new perspective allows us to accept them and to work with the dynamics of the challenge so that it becomes an opportunity for growth.

Face deep patterns explores the challenge we have when patterns from our childhood and our parents resurface unconsciously. Through facing them we bring the possibility of rewiring.

Relax into the unknown invites us to accept the unknown future we step into.

Love your new body brings this acceptance home to ourselves and our own body, loving and cherishing our new physical self alongside our internal changes.

Dare to say 'No' asks us to place healthy boundaries that allow us to honour our new priorities.

Motherhood is a more than full time role which can leave us emotionally, mentally and physically exhausted: **It's good to do nothing** reminds us of the importance of just being and recharging.

You are your own anchor gives us a sense of ownership over our Mother's

Journey and a reminder that we can give ourselves the support, grounding and nourishment that we need.

There are so many ways that we might not live up to our own standards, ideals and expectations, and yet we are the best mother for our children: **You are good enough** helps support us to have positive internal dialogue that reinforces our sense of worth as a mother.

Transform

The Transform family explores the process of personal transformation and some tools we can use to support this.

Connect with your roots and ancestors reminds us that we are part of a lineage of mothers that have passed down wisdom, patterns and stories.

Create something and you will discover ways to explore your feelings and your personal transformation journey.

You are a leader reminds us that becoming a mother brings us into a leadership position in our family, through feminine leadership we can support and guide our children.

Let go of assumptions, expectations and judgements. Letting go allows us to be fully present with what is, rather than what might have been.

Birthing is your initiation is an indication of the profound journey we went through that brought us into motherhood.

Open to emergence calls us to open our minds, hearts and arms to the unexpected, unfolding journey ahead.

With the **Meet the Goddess** principle we connect with the sacred and cosmic energies within us and surrounding us.

Empower

Mothering takes a lot of our resources and we need to find ways to recharge and nourish and empower ourselves. The Empower family of principles focuses on how to create opportunities for self-care, community support and being proactive with our life path.

Listen to our bodies, our children, our partners, ourselves. Through listening we come into connection and nourishment.

Practice self-care with your child allows us to meet our self-care needs without yearning after some unachievable golden time without our children.

Give gratitude supports us to be present and humble and connect with the beauty around us.

Each of us can benefit from support at times, however other people may not be aware of the need or how to help so we need to **Ask for help and be proactive**.

Nourish community demonstrates how friendships and community are like gardens and need attention and nurturing.

Trust your intuition signifies the importance of connecting with ourselves, and feeling into what is right for us and for our children.

Design your life path is a call to observe, vision, plan and be proactive with what you want to manifest in your life.

Nourish Your Gifts

The Nourish Your Gifts family highlights some of the many skills and qualities mothers have. Motherhood can also lead us to new unexpected qualities.

Find your strength is an invitation to tap into your resources and build on them: as mothers we are stretched in many ways that increase our strength daily.

Motherhood is Joy reminds us of the honour and the joy of being such an intimate and vital part of another person's life. Motherhood can widen our capacity for love, joy and connection.

Your gift is effectiveness is an affirmation of our ability for our effectiveness to grow as we juggle the multitude of mothering duties, let alone outside work and other commitments.

Embrace your vulner-ability calls for us to be human and not be perfect. To see our vulnerability as an ability that can open unexpected doors.

Become self-aware invites us to walk the never ending path of self discovery and self-awareness, tutored by our children, our greatest teachers.

Receive the gift of patience is an invitation to open up to empathy, love and compassion, and to nourish our emotional intelligence.

Embrace your feminine power is an opportunity to reconnect to our bodies and our deeper being, fully embracing our new role in this world.

Connect with Nature

Nature – also known as the more than human world – has deep, profound wisdom from billions of years of evolution. The family of Connect With Nature is an invitation to be guided, supported, nourished, inspired and refreshed through deep nature connection. It can support us as mothers, as well as providing vital nourishment for our children.

Get out, get wild is an invitation to step outside and see what happens.

You are nature reminds us that every part of us is part of nature.

Your child is your nature mentor represents the benefits we receive when we tune into our children's natural sense of awe, wonder and curiosity.

Care for Earth reminds us that as mothers we come into a greater sense of responsibility to care for Earth and for future generations.

The principle of **Ground Yourself** shows us how the elements of fire, earth, water and air can support us.

Connect with the plant world expresses the many different ways in which the plant world can bring benefits to the emotional and physical health of ourselves and our children.

Align with natural patterns and cycles directs our attention to the natural patterns and cycles that can support and energise us when we observe and find balance with them.

THE JOURNEY

*'It is by going down into the abyss that we recover the treasures of life.
Where you stumble, there lies your treasure.
The very cave you are afraid to enter turns out to be the source of what you are looking for.'*

Joseph Campbell

LISTEN TO THE CALL

Becoming a mother is your rite of passage
·
Be brave and your helpers will appear
·
Motherhood is your pathway to grow

Your story as a mother is a unique story of adventures, hardships and joy. A tale of personal growth, development and transformation.

Thumbelina, the *Princess and the Frog*, *Cinderella*, the good girl in *Mother Holle*, Dorothy in the *Wizard of Oz* and *Alice in Wonderland* are all familiar to us. The heroine receives a call and leaves behind the ordinary world of the past. Initiated to a new stage of life, she goes through a journey of trials facing great dangers on her way. At the end of her adventures she finally returns home with her elixir, her true gift. By the end of the story her personality is completely transformed and she becomes a more mature person, she finds her true self and mission in life.

Traditional Earth-based cultures acknowledge transitions from one human life stage to another and formed collective rituals. As women we live a cyclical life. Our first menstruation is a crossing from being a girl to becoming a fertile woman. Our first childbirth marks the threshold from the phase of being a woman to becoming a mother. With wisdom and age women cease to menstruate, and cross into the season of elder women in their full power. As nowadays we live much longer than our ancestors, there is a potential to spend a good few years in our last phase of life, when our accumulated wisdom could serve others. With each phase of life there is a rite of passage that marks the end of one stage and brings about a new one. These initiations ensure that we, as women are reborn again and again to fully live each stage of our lives.

Reflective questions

What life event was your passage from being a girl to becoming a woman?

Can you remember your call to become a mother?

If you look at your mother journey so far, what is the most meaningful thing you have learnt?

Activity

Draw a circular drawing of your life journey (including the period you have lived and life ahead of you), and mark the life stages you have lived: what were the most meaningful lessons? Mark the stages ahead of you: what are your aspirations for those life stages?

CROSS THE THRESHOLD

Celebrate who you were as a maiden

·

Birthing is your initiation

·

Give birth to yourself as a mother

In a famous fairy tale, the young princess is playing in the garden with her golden globe. Suddenly the ball falls into the spring water, a frog appears offering his service to the princess. The frog marks the end of a life stage and the beginning of a new one. Childhood ends and her transformative journey towards adulthood begins. If you are a mother now, you probably had a turning point some years back. At that point your familiar life with family, work, friends, roles, jobs somehow became outgrown, and you started your journey towards motherhood. Stepping from maiden to mother does not start with the childbirth, even if birthing is a definite threshold to cross over.

Crossing a threshold is as much an emotional and mental transition as it is a physical event. Understanding that giving birth is a rite of passage, gives meaning to the huge emotional and physical change that happens with childbirth. When we understand it as a rite of passage, we can recognise the transformation from Maiden to Mother. The childbearing year is a journey of separation from our previous lives during the nine months of pregnancy, transformation with childbirth and reintegration during the period of postpartum. A journey hugely influenced by ever changing hormones, emotions and the constant change experienced in our body. In the midst of all that change we need emotional and financial stability, full support from our partners (if we have them), families and friends. As mothers we also need to be cared for so that we can nurture our children.

Each one of our childbirths can take us deeper into the experience of motherhood, as every birth and every child is unique. We can also discover ourselves as having a different mothering relationship with each of our children.

Reflective questions

What did you leave behind when you transitioned from maiden to mother?

What did you gain and what did you lose?

If you met your maiden self now, what would be your message to her?

Activity

Can you recall the woman you knew yourself to be, before you became a mother? Draw a picture of yourself, visualising the most valuable gifts you had as a young woman. Think about the skills, special competencies and anything you feel was special in you then. These are resources you can use now as a mother.

BEFRIEND YOUR DRAGONS

Accept help and reach out for support

Find community with other mothers

Surround yourself with supportive people

Listen to your inner voice when making decisions

Being a mother might be the most challenging, most complex and most influential role of our lives. Suddenly there are so many new tasks and new decisions we need to make, and there's a baby we need to look after.

In the story of Mother Holle, the good girl falls into a well and finds herself in a strange dreamlike land, where everything is unfamiliar, and she has to go through a series of trials. Similarly, we find ourselves in unknown territory, and have no map for Motherland. Our map emerges as we go along and face unexpected challenges. These trials show us that our initiation to motherhood has begun. In fairy tales heroines often receive supernatural help. Dorothy is helped by the Good Witch of the North. Ms. Fieldmouse, a hospitable mouse lady takes Thumbelina into her warm home when winter arrives. Just like all these characters in the stories, we as mothers need to be courageous and we need to surround ourselves with supportive people.

In folk tales, the trials of the journey are often symbolised by dragons. The hero fights them, finally cutting off the head of the dragon. What does the heroine do? She befriends the dragons. When it comes to stress, instead of getting ready to fight or to flee, women are more likely to befriend the enemy and to seek support from other people. We need allies on our mothering journey, we need to meet mothers and friends and accept help from family members. Befriending our dragons involves finding balance between being a mother and being a part of our community.

Reflective questions

Can you identify a helper in your early motherhood trials- someone real or a symbolic figure – who has helped you in challenging times?

Can you recall a time as a new mother when you really needed advice, support and someone was there: a mentor, an ally, a family member or a health professional who fulfilled this role?

Activity

Create some 'me-time', and prepare your favourite colour pencils or paints (or borrow your children's). Make a picture of your dragon: what do/did you find the most challenging part of becoming/being a mother? What would your dragons be called? How would you befriend or tame them?

BE WITH THE DARKNESS

Ask for help and be proactive
·
Nurture yourself, practice self-care
·
Use the healing power of nature
·
Sleep and rest whenever you can

Some of the biggest challenges new mothers face may be unresolved childbirth experience, insecurities and lack of information about childcare, social isolation, financial and emotional instability, physical exhaustion and sleep deprivation. We are not alone anymore and we cannot run away from being a mother. We are required to cope with stress and re-organise our lives. For some mothers childbirth was so traumatic that it can take months or even years to recover. It may be heartbreakingly difficult in the first weeks to find a real connection to our baby. Or we might have lost this connection in a miscarriage and we feel we cannot move through our grief. We may be struggling with the everyday challenges of being a mother, or being a single mother. Mothers face a unique set of challenges, as well as each mother having their own individual challenges.

A symbolic image repeated in ancient myths is the 'belly of the whale', an archetype of death and rebirth. Being in the belly of the whale is a time and place of not knowing, a time of asking and not answering. It may feel like living the 'dark night of the soul', an expression derived from a medieval poem describing the journey of the soul in the unknown. This is a time of suffering with seemingly no hope of release. Feeling turned inside out. At some point we may give up trying to be rescued and we let go of the stories about how we imagined this part of our lives. We let go of old expectations from others, of images of ourselves that no longer serve us. Pain is often labelled as negative, when in fact, it can be an impetus for change. The desire to stop the pain can actually be the thing that enables us to move.

Reflective questions

*Have you been in the 'belly of the whale', a dark hole of motherhood?
What did it look like? What did it feel like?
What was the most difficult point, the darkest point of insecurity?
What did you really need when you were in this place?
What support and guidance did you receive?*

Activity

Making a mistake is still widely understood as a failure. Instead, we can see our mistakes as opportunities to rethink and recreate our choices in life. Let us introduce you to the concept of the art of flipping. What do we flip? Hardship to opportunity, crisis to potential. Every coin has two sides: what looks like a challenge on one side, might be an opportunity from the other side. The art is in looking at both sides.

Take a pen and your journal or a sheet of paper. Write down the most challenging part of your motherhood at the moment – in a full sentence using 'I' and present tense. Then think about what this situation is teaching you, how can this challenge become an opportunity. See the other side and think: what could I learn from this challenge, what could it teach me, or show me? Who do I become when I get through this hardship? Write it down below the previous one, also using present tense.

9

FIND YOUR ELIXIR

Accept your gifts of motherhood

Acknowledge and celebrate your lessons as a mother

Welcome and integrate your new skills

All of us, as women, are Goddesses; it is our true nature. Through giving birth, you become the vessel for new life to arrive, and your creative force manifests. Your body softens to accommodate and nurture your baby. Your personality softens so that you can care for your child. Our softness is like the grass in a windy meadow: soft and strong at the same time. It has to be both to enable us to withstand the unexpected challenges inherent in our new role. Like Dorothy meeting the Wizard of Oz for the second time, we are about to discover the essence of what we learnt since we set off on the yellow brick road. We have come so far on our path through Motherland. We may feel greatly empowered by the experience of giving birth, creating and sustaining a new life, adapting to the changed circumstances and withstanding challenges. We may emerge from our trials and hardships a hundred times stronger than we felt before. We discover new sides of ourselves, new skills we were not aware of before. The process of birthing creates a huge potential for every woman to grow and thrive.

Motherhood is a transformative time. Connecting with our strength in a supportive environment can boost our confidence and creativity. We need creativity and responsibility for child rearing. Our ability to take responsibility shifts greatly, our personality matures. What we learn from being a mother is palpable in the family, it expands to all members. We may experience a positive shift in our conflict resolution skills, prioritising, setting boundaries and organising our daily tasks. Not to mention the ability to truly, unconditionally love another being.

Reflective questions

What are your most important gifts from motherhood?

What have you learnt since you became a mother?

Which sides of you are shining more brightly since you became a mother?

Activity

Find a daily affirmation and say it out loud several times a day. Either choose a principle from the Nourish Your Gifts family, or make up your own affirmation; what is the gift you are ready to claim, to embrace from your motherhood? 'Find Your Strength', 'Motherhood Is Joy', 'Your Gift Is Effectiveness', 'Embrace Your Vulner-ability', 'Become Self-aware', 'Receive The Gift Of Patience', 'Embrace Your Feminine Power'.

If you have the Mother Nature Card Deck, pick one of the cards, place it on your altar, near your bed or deck, dashboard or in your journal. You can reword the principle in the first person and present tense to create an affirmation for yourself.

MAKE PEACE WITH YOUR SHADOW

See darkness and light as one

See your dark side as an integral part of you

Set yourself on your path towards self-liberation

Nourish, love and heal your inner child

When our children push our buttons, triggering unresolved emotions, it is time to face our old dysfunctional patterns.

Holding repressed anger of sibling rivalry as a child, will make it hard to be there for our bickering children. It is time to do something about your anger: go back to your childhood memories, feel the rage in your body, shout it out loud, talk to your adult sibling.

Growing up as an anxious child, the one standing alone in a quiet corner might be a remote memory. Seeing your child going through the same thing can evoke your pain and can push you to face these memories, now with a mature personality.

We all carry an inner child within, a wounded little one who carries pain, anger and sadness. This child and her suffering is repressed most of the time in our unconscious. Still, any unpleasant events, unexpected reactions, and especially the behaviour of our children may bring her to the surface in a split second. We may find ways to mother the part of us that is still a wounded little girl as we transform from daughter to mother. We might want to talk to her, tell her it is alright, there is no danger, she is safe, loved and looked after. We might want to say to her: those times are over, we have grown up and we are able to protect her. At times when having a walk with our children outdoors, let's invite our inner child to join us. Let's invite her to play with us and our children. Support your child in fearful, painful times, then recognise and celebrate success. Invite your inner child to celebrate with you!

Reflective questions

What are your dark sides you would prefer not to see?

What wounds do you wish to heal to enable you to be the best mother you can be?

In what ways could you love and nurture your inner child?

Activity

Write down the ways of parenting from your mother and father that you would like to leave behind. What are your alternative ways of caring, mentoring and lovingly putting boundaries into place for your own children?

COME INTO ALIGNMENT

Realign your life path as a mother

Celebrate the extraordinariness of your ordinary life

Create the culture you want with your family

In myths and folk tales the heroine emerges from the extraordinary world of trials and is ready to bring back her elixir to the world. Is the heroine able to go back and serve her community? Are we able to benefit from the new sides of our personality as mothers in other walks of life? Can we be more patient with our extended family? Can we accept colleagues looking after their personal sustainability just as we have learned to look after ourselves? Are we able to bring the quality of being rather than doing into our everyday life? Can we stand up for ourselves at work just as we do for our children? Are we able to set boundaries? Can we love and accept unconditionally our fellow human beings just as we love our child?

Now our culture as a mother becomes more established. This is where everything makes sense again, we are used to our daily routines, our new way of seeing the world and our place in it. Mothers become skilled in bridging two worlds, our mother microculture and society's macroculture. We integrate our feminine and masculine sides, the nurturing BEING part and the active, outgoing DOING part. This is the completion of one stage on our spiral path, a place we may pass many times as we progress on our Mother's Journey.

Motherhood is a spiritual path. Sitting and meditating alone in a cave might be challenging, but what about staying present and loving with our children and family twenty-four seven?! This really is a path towards self actualisation.

Reflective questions

What are you claiming as your true self as a mother?

How can you make your everyday life fulfilling?

How can you nurture all parts of you that are important?

What are your next steps as a mother?

Activity

List your most valuable gifts of motherhood, new skills, new parts of yourself that you developed or discovered as a mother.

Now think about how can you use them in other walks of your life.

How could these new competencies support you in your roles in the wider community?

REFRAME CHALLENGES

'In the underworld there is no sense of time, time is endless and you cannot rush your stay.'

Maureen Murdock, *The Heroine's Journey*

FACE DEEP PATTERNS

Talk to your mother about your childhood

Find someone who can truly listen

Get to know your shadows

Find a loving way to set boundaries for your child

'I can't believe I just said THAT!' When we become mothers, old behavioural patterns can surface. We can hear our mother's long-forgotten words slipping out of our mouths. We are not alone anymore, no pain, sadness or anger can be hidden. We cannot pretend in front of our children. Yes, they mirror old wounds, and push those buttons that still feel painful. We are faced with an opportunity to rewrite deeply seated ways of being and reacting. We have been protecting ourselves by blocking these feelings. Now, when our emotional balance would be most needed, old wounds are torn apart and we have no clue on how to react. Facing old patterns and becoming self-aware of our less desirable sides are the first steps towards accepting our shadows. The two sides of the Mother are visible in dreams and folktales: the good, nurturing, sustaining mother and the evil, dark, punishing mother, the wicked witch. These images became archetypes, powerful symbolic images in our collective human unconscious. With our children we can actually become those two aspects in our everyday life: we are loving and nurturing most of the time, and at other times we can't hide becoming angry and frustrated, as much as we may try. In our rage our children might experience the disruptive nature of the Dark Mother. When we understand that we embody both sides, we gain a new perspective; we bring those two sides together. Through self examination and introspection we can gain self awareness and we can integrate our shadows. Light and dark sides come into alignment again. When we heal this split, we enable integration and personal growth.

Reflective questions

What are the patterns you don't want to carry on from your mother; things you want to do differently in your role as a mother?

What are the things that she did well that you do want to pass on to your children?

Activity

Write a journal of the most emotionally challenging situations with your child. Write down your emotional states every day, and note every single incident when you lost your temper or were really challenged by your child's behaviour. Keep the journal for a week, writing down: the day, your general emotional state on that day, and each incident, including what happened and your feelings about your child at that time. What are the overall patterns? Can you see similarities? What could you do differently?

RELAX INTO THE UNKNOWN

Trust the unfolding path

·

Embrace change as your ally

·

Be comfortable with pattern disruption

·

Let go of automatic pilot

Parenting is a whole new world of experiences, perspectives and situations. There are so many choices about parenting and constant decisions to make, from the significant ones to the numerous everyday ones. Navigating all of the options can be overwhelming at times. However, we can't know all the ripples of any decision we make or what the consequences would be if we had made a different decision at any point. Therefore, we need to learn to relax with all these unknowns and variables and trust the unfolding path.

Becoming a mother is one of the biggest pattern disruptions that we will experience in our lives. All of our patterns can be thrown out of the window – our eating, sleeping, exercise, and self-care patterns become unrecognisable to what they once were. Even our thinking patterns shift. This can be quite disorientating and ungrounding, but it does invite us to shift from any cultural conditioning and patterns on automatic pilot and give space for new patterns and ideas to take root. Our child has no concept of time and the rules of life that we play by as adults, so we need to adjust to their pace of life, and accept these new unknown patterns. Pattern disruption and stepping into the unknown is a constant in a mother's life, as our children and their needs, routines and characteristics shift. We can embrace change as our ally, and know that something new is just around the corner.

Reflective questions

What patterns have changed for you since becoming a mother?

Which part of your body could you invite to relax into the unknown?

Activity

Try some active pattern disruption to practice relaxing into the unknown and letting go of conditioning. Try brushing your teeth with your other hand, walking faster or eating slower.
Reflect on how this feels.

LOVE YOUR NEW BODY

Your body is your home

·

See the beauty in your changed shape

·

Create space for rituals to nurture your body

We are bombarded by media images of how a perfect, fit female body should look. We are conditioned to try to be slim, sporty and seductive, and the beauty industry suggests we maintain that shape for a lifetime. We call you to believe you shouldn't! We call you to believe that your body is perfect already, in its own uniquely beautiful way. Nature has its own timing and cycles: it is alive. Our body is changing together with our soul. Change is natural – it is experience, it is wisdom. Change is personal growth. Yes, your body changed. It brought a child into the world. Pregnancy might be the first time we get closely in touch with our womb. This mysterious organ is left unnoticed by many of us until it starts to grow to accommodate our baby. Our body and our womb work hand in hand during labour to bring the baby into the world.

During pregnancy, your body experienced the most profound union: one of a mother and a child. You experienced the wisdom of your body, it knew exactly how to develop two united cells into a fully grown baby, it knew how to give birth, how to feed and how to care for your child. Your touch, intimacy and love in a sensual form are important for the development of your child. And yes, apart from being mothers, we are still women. We can look at our changed body shape and scars with a loving attitude. Grieve your old shape, cry out all the tears you have about your scar, your belly, your breasts, then get in deep touch with your new shape. Find little self-love rituals, make them part of your me-time, give yourself a warm oil massage, have a regular swim, sauna, stay in bed on Sunday mornings, get naked in nature. Feeling beautiful and graceful is your birthright!

Reflective questions

How has your image of yourself as a woman changed since you became a mother?

What does beauty mean to you?

In what ways is your body beautiful, just like the rest of nature?

Activity

Find an occasion to be naked in nature. Bathe in the sea, get dirty with earth, roll in the sand, walk in the fields; find your beauty by experiencing yourself as part of Mother Nature.

You are nature: find some time alone; and get naked – having a shower can be a great time for this.

Look at yourself naked in the mirror. Take a good look at yourself and let your eyes and hands gently appreciate your amazing body that created life.

DARE TO SAY NO

Saying no is saying yes to healthy boundaries
·
Be crystal clear on your boundaries
·
Stop feeling guilty about saying 'No'

Are you a 'yes' person? Do you say yes to extra work and events, to more and more projects, to your family requests (even if your plate is already full)? Being a 'yes' person can be exhausting and tiring if we haven't set healthy boundaries.

Being a mother encourages us to learn the power of saying 'no.' Suddenly our priorities change, shifting to make sure our children are healthy, keeping routines and having consistent nap times and bedtimes. We may start saying no to outings that conflict with our nap times and bedtimes, saying no to people visiting if they are sick, saying no to people feeding our child sweets and saying no to things that stop our family from spending quality time together. As we become mothers we need to learn to set healthy boundaries and listen to our internal self, and not make ourselves and our child available to everyone, all the time.

Boundaries allow us to take better care of ourselves – emotionally, mentally and physically. Setting boundaries can apply to any aspect of your life – personal time, personal beliefs, family, work and friends.

You alone are responsible for showing others how they can treat you by deciding what you will and won't accept. Setting boundaries doesn't make you a bad or selfish person – it makes you a whole and healthy person who is striving for balance and happiness.

Reflective questions

Can you recognise when you are doing something out of obligation or to please others?

How do you set healthy boundaries?

What boundaries would you like to put in place in your life to create a happier, healthier environment for you and your family?

Activity

Stand in front of the mirror and smile at yourself.

Recognise the gentleness in your eyes, curves of your lips, lines around your face. Now think about a situation where you recognise your boundaries are being pushed. Can you say no to it? Say 'no' loudly and observe how your face changes. Is your gesture firm and solid? Would you believe somebody if they said 'no' like this?

Can you express your boundary with grace without pointing to others, but merely expressing your truth? Practice saying no in different ways.

As you finish, smile at yourself again.

IT'S GOOD TO DO NOTHING

Just be

Experience the present moment

Rest and relax

Treasure stillness and silence

Motherhood is a full and rich experience that can leave little time for anything else. It is tempting to fill the small gaps in our day with other things, such as housework and computer time. But we don't need to fill every moment of day and night. Tune in to the rest and active cycles and rhythms of your children and take time while your child is sleeping to rest, sleep and do nothing. We can allow the gaps to be filled with emptiness, silence and stillness. Recharging and rejuvenating benefits everyone. These moments of nothing encourage our nervous system to destress and unwind, and we can feel the benefits on a cellular level. Our thoughts have time and space to settle and our emotions have space to surface. Doing nothing is an opportunity to practice mindfulness and bring ourselves into the present moment. Silence and stillness are powerful ways to connect with ourselves. Surrender to tiredness and just sleep. Recharge whenever you can. Doing nothing has multiple benefits for our bodies, our minds and our emotions.

Reflective questions

When was the last time you sat and did nothing?

What were the messages you were given as a child about doing nothing?

What are the thoughts that stop you doing nothing?

Activity

Do nothing – for just ten minutes. Just sit or lie down and be. You can be on the sofa or bed or out in nature.

Bring yourself into the present moment.

Notice any tensions that arise in you, thinking about other things that you could be doing.

At the end of the ten minutes reflect upon your body – does it feel different? Notice your mind and thoughts – What has changed?

Try to make this a daily practice of having at least ten minutes a day of doing nothing.

YOU ARE YOUR OWN ANCHOR

Be still and listen inwards

Trust that the chaos will give birth to clarity

See your strength in your weakness

See your hardship as an opportunity

New mothers often spend a lot of the day alone with their child at home. We miss adult relationships and quality time with friends. We need to make many decisions when health visitors, doctors, grandparents, internet sites and parenting books provide conflicting information. Suddenly we face many new questions, much more financial expenditure and a lot less income. Relationships can loosen in the midst of struggles with unexpected challenges, conflicting values, ideas and priorities. Unstable relationships combined with financial difficulties may lead to parents breaking up. For single mothers financial struggle is a big challenge.

Being in the state of not-knowing, in a time of chaos or crisis is unsettling. We can lose ourselves in it. You may figure out which things in life you can change and which you cannot. And those you cannot, you learn to accept. The benefit of acceptance is that you change your attitude towards the unchangeable, and free up the energy you used for fighting. Try this: you can let go of struggling against struggling. When we let go of our struggle, we can rest peacefully in what is actually happening. We need to consult our inner knowing to find the solution that works for us. A valuable mantra is: 'I take refuge in my inner knowing'.

Reflective questions

What can you let go of to make it easier for you?

How can you create supportive relationships around you?

Who are the people that make you feel stronger?

Who are the people you can rely on and can help you to let go of being strong?

Activity

Create some undisturbed time for yourself (half an hour while your child sleeps is perfect). Create a nice atmosphere, light a candle and put on relaxing quiet music. Sit comfortably with your spine straight. Let your eyes close. Be still and focus on your breath for a few minutes (notice your in-breath and your out-breath, its rhythm and pace). Visualise yourself standing still and strong in the midst of a storm. Change the volume and the strength of the storm; see the challenging life events whirling up and around in the storm and see yourself standing still in the midst of it. Hold the image of yourself withstanding the storm strong and tall, and hold this image in front of your closed eyelids.

See this image floating away from your perspective, then come back to your physical environment with your full attention.

YOU ARE GOOD ENOUGH

Transform your guilt

·

Look at what works well

·

Use positive reinforcement

·

Find people who tell you 'Yes, you can!'

Guilt is one of the biggest dragons we face as mothers. Because we know how important these first years of childhood are, we want to do our best. We want to provide a strong emotional foundation for our children, and sometimes we can become extreme in our striving to be a good mother. Mothers all over the globe struggle with the feeling that they are not 'good enough', that they are doing something wrong. They are blaming themselves for being too impatient, not keeping a daily routine, for stopping or for continuing breastfeeding, for sleeping with or without their children, not playing enough with them, putting on the TV when feeling too tired to be present with their child, needing to work when they would rather be with their child, reacting too emotionally, not being able to calm their child down; the list is endless.

Depending on our cultural expectations there are ideas about what a 'good mother' is like: she is satisfied by simply being at home and taking care of her children, letting go of all her previous aspirations, whilst at the other end of the scale, there is the image of the working woman going back to the office six weeks after giving birth. If we try to live up to any of these extreme expectations, we will most likely fail. Coming to terms with where we are in life, can support us to find balance and be happy. Feeding different parts of our personalities helps us to thrive. Acceptance is the antidote for guilt. Accepting who we are, what we do, how we respond. Giving and receiving praise and gratitude in our families supports everyone to increase their self-worth and satisfaction with themselves and life.

Yes, you are good enough!

Reflective questions

What are you doing well?

In what ways is your love toward your children expressed daily?

In what ways are you a great mother?

What support do you need so that you can be your best?

Activity

Look at your BIGGEST DRAGON, your 'fault', the thing you most frequently beat yourself up about. Write it down clearly with big letters, on an A4 paper. Now, turn the page upside down (literally do it!). Then think about: 'How could this thing become my ally? What is the positive quality that lies underneath the negative statement? What is the strength within this weakness? What is the opportunity within this problem?' Write it down. Turn this into an 'I' statement using the present tense. E.g. I am structured. Now you have got your affirmation. Use it as a mantra, say it out loud several times a day, upon waking up and before going to bed.

TRANSFORM

'Finding out about being instead of doing is the sacred task of the Feminine . . . And our planet, Gaia needs this wisdom, of mindful being to get into a right relationship with all living being. Our endless doing has created incredible destruction to the Earth.'

Maureen Murdock, *The Heroine's Journey*

CONNECT WITH YOUR ROOTS AND ANCESTORS

Connect with your female lineage

·

Celebrate the wisdom of your ancestors

·

Make peace with your mother

Our first memories are stored from the time we spent in our mother's womb. The first nine months and important events during our mother's pregnancy are said to form the basis of our unconscious. This deep imprint will influence our behaviour and actions. Conversely, when we become pregnant, our womb-dweller sends new cells through the placenta that are also then stored in our body. Apart from these cells, half of the genetic information of our future grandchildren already resides inside our womb, in the developing body of our child. Emotions like joy and sadness, imprints of important life events may be stored as information in our cellular memory and go on to be inherited by our children, grandchildren and great-great grandchildren.

Our lives are intertwined in many ways with our ancestors and our offspring. It is an unbroken chain of information. Native American tribes hold dear the concept of planning for seven generations, acknowledging that the impact of any decisions should be considered for seven generations into the future.

From daughter we transform into a mother. Parenting can bring us into situations where we reconnect with our inner child, facing our old wounds or reliving childhood joys. While learning to mother our children, we are also learning to mother ourselves from within, by taking care of our inner child and any unmet childhood needs. Being transformed from daughter to mother also means we may look at our mother differently. Understanding her at a deeper level may bring healing to challenging mother-daughter relationships. Find a way to connect with your roots, understand your mother and your grandmother – see them in the midst of the historical events they lived within, and celebrate their lives.

Reflective questions

Where are your roots?

What is your heritage from your female ancestors?

What are you grateful to your mother for?

Activity

Create an 'altar' of your female lineage. Find pictures, old photographs, relics from your mother, grandmother, great grandmother and great-great grandmother, as long back as you can. You may be able to put them in one big frame and place it somewhere visible in your home. Talk to your children about their ancestors. Light a candle once in a while – maybe on Mother's Day and other significant days – to celebrate their lives and the wisdom that came through them.

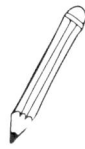

CREATE SOMETHING

Create something, anything

Put aside your inner critic

Express emotions through creativity

Be creative with your child

We can use creativity as a way of connecting with ourselves – to heal, to express, to understand, to relax, to discover, to give us energy and to release and move stagnant energy. There are many forms of creative expression; artwork, doodles, playing with colour, the clothes we wear, homemaking, cooking, gardening, music, poetry, writing, conversations, pottery, sculpting, playing with clay, storytelling, making fires, woodwork, handwriting, dancing. Through creative expression healing, motivation, community, insights, connection, joy and vitality can emerge. Allow the ever-changing circumstances of your life as a mother to bring fresh ideas and creative flow. Being creative and making things is part of our human nature. It is part of the lineage of human culture through time, from making fire, to making tools, to creating language.

Creativity is part of our evolutionary blueprint. As we become mothers it can be challenging to find time, energy and space to be creative. We may need to let go of previous methods of expression that are time consuming, detailed or have inappropriate materials. We may need to find new ways to flow with our creativity that fit in with or around our children. One of the gifts though, for our creativity is our children and their endless imagination, their delight in colours and texture and the ample opportunities they provide us with for play. We can find ways to meet our needs and their needs for creative expression simultaneously. Creativity enables us to express grief and sadness and find joy and happiness.

Reflective questions

What times of day, week or month do you naturally feel creative?

What ways are you already creative?

How is creativity already present in your work, family, hobbies, childbearing, and mundane tasks?

Activity

Get out some finger paints and play with them. Use your fingers, your toes, your elbows – get messy.

Paint your journey through motherhood – be abstract and intuitive, playful and free.

YOU ARE A LEADER

Acknowledge your profound influence

Act with purpose

Accept your leadership role

As a mother we take responsibility for our children. It is worth acknowledging that a mother's influence on her family is profound. We are guiding and leading our families, although this requires us to redefine leadership. A direct style of leadership can be confrontational, although sometimes necessary, usually though, a more subtle approach is needed for our families. We are encouraging and facilitating them. We can give our children opportunities and experiences that allow their gifts to surface. Our leadership includes anticipating the consequences and trying to mitigate any unpleasant ones. Our leadership as mothers involves a soft power and nurturing guidance. There are many ways to take leadership in our families; with food choices, supporting friendships, choosing schools and activities. Leadership involves organisation, making plans and decisions and following that through into action.

We are responsible for finding ways to meet all of the family's needs. Accepting our leadership means we can act with purpose. With our feet on the ground and wide angled vision we can forge pathways for our growing children. We are role models for our children for how to be, act and interact in the world using our full power.

Reflective questions

What are your beliefs around leadership?

What does feminine or masculine leadership mean to you?

In what ways do you embody leadership?

Activity

Music can be a guide to many different places within us. Use music to help you embody different qualities of leadership. Please note that we don't say any quality is better than the other, they are just different and we are able to use each in the best possible way when appropriate. Depending on how much time you have, select a few songs that have different rhythm, instruments, lyrics etc. Put on the first song and invite your body to relax and express freely as the music is playing. Then put on a song that is more structured and let your body dance to it. Observe how it feels.

What qualities is the music evoking in your body? You can try out several songs or go directly to a song that is gentle and flowing.

Let your body show you an embodiment of a different kind of leadership.

LET GO

Let go of your maiden self

Let go of perfectionism

Be gentle with yourself

Stepping into motherhood requires letting go of our maiden self to fully accept our mother self. It is time to embrace pattern disruption and let go of previous day to day habits, routines and patterns. Be gentle with yourself. Each mother and every child has their own journey to make, let go of all expectations. Let go of assumptions, comparisons, struggles and desires. And most of all let go of perfectionism. Allow your Mother Journey to unfold. Allow your children to develop into themselves. There is no point comparing yourself to other mothers, or your child to other children: each person is unique.

There is much for a mother to consider and many choices to make. At times it can be overwhelming and we can be unsure whether we have made the right choices. Every day, every moment could have been different. We could have said, done, felt different things, not better or worse – just different. However, we can never know the consequences of our actions or decisions over time. Let go of trying to make the 'right' decision.

Let go of negative self talk, or saying 'I'm not . . .', 'I can't . . .,' 'I didn't . . .', 'I should have . . .' Instead value your strengths and the effort and thought you are putting into making choices. Talk kindly to yourself. Letting go creates space for letting in – letting in our gifts as mothers.

Reflective questions

What expectations of yourself could you let go of?

What parts of your maiden self did you let go of?

In what situations are you really hard on yourself? Recognise that you have done the best you could in that moment and be gentle with yourself.

Activity

Bring self awareness to your internal and external dialogue.

When are you using the word 'should'? Whenever you notice yourself using should, say the sentence again with a could (either internally or out loud). Notice the difference that makes to your feelings, your body, your approach to any next steps.

BIRTHING IS YOUR INITIATION

Your body has all the wisdom it needs

Another life has come through you

You truly have become part of the mystery of life

You can fully trust your body

Women are capable of giving birth. Our body is biologically designed for that and is perfectly capable of doing it. We have simple needs during labour: to feel safe, to be in a warm place with gentle lights, to be silent, to have people around who we trust. After forty weeks of tuning into each other with your baby, you have established a connection for a lifetime. Your body becomes a vessel for the newborn to arrive. Your hormones, tissues and bones are working hand in hand to bring this new life into the world. We are physical beings, our animal instincts take the lead during labour, and the human part of our brain switches off.

Giving birth can be seen as one of the universal, mysterious gateways of existence. When we give birth, we encounter Life and Death, the gateway opens up and disappears. We have the unique experience of greeting a soul to this earthly experience.

The way in which a newborn arrives to this world has a long-term influence on the child, mother and the whole family. A smooth and beautiful experience sets a positive scene and helps create a harmonious postnatal period. On the other hand, having had a difficult or traumatic birth does not mean that the journey is on a bad track for good. There are many ways we can work through our painful memories and rewrite our childbirth story for a harmonious continuation.

Reflective questions

What was the most magical thing about the birth of your child?

Can you recall the first time you looked into your child's eyes?

What transformed or changed within you after the birth of your child, and how can that strengthen you as a mother?

Activity

Do this practice, especially if you feel you still have work to do about your childbirth experience. Talk to someone about your childbirth, someone you know and feel safe with; a good friend, another mother you know well, your doula, your mother, your partner or a counsellor/therapist.

Make this conversation a planned occasion, when you have a good two hours uninterrupted. Tell your story freely with your own words, talking about your experience including facts and also your feelings about them.

When you speak, make sure you talk about these things: 'The way I planned to give birth was . . .' 'The way I gave birth was . . .' 'Feelings I hold about this experience are . . .'

OPEN TO EMERGENCE

Open to the unfolding journey

Welcome the unexpected and unpredictable

Be aware of what is arising

Allow challenge to bring new and surprising gifts

Life is spontaneous and miraculous and we become aware of this in a more profound, embodied way than ever before when we are pregnant, give birth and become a mother. The transformation we undergo when we become mothers can be deeply profound and surprising, even unbelievable at times. Emergence is when new things emerge, arise, come into being – birth. From birth a mother emerges – an entirely new person. When things interact and combine new and unexpected possibilities arise. It is through the emergent process of the Mother's Journey, through the challenges and leaving behind our maiden selves, that new skills, qualities, gifts and talents appear in us. It is not just qualities that have lain hidden in us, it can be entirely new and unexpected elixirs that emerge. With fertile emergence love, compassion, appreciation, our life's purpose and connection can come to light. There is the potential for healing, community, solidarity and insights to emerge when we connect with others.

With an open heart, mind and arms we can open to emergence and be observant to what wants to come through, to what is arising in the moment.

Opening to emergence is a hopeful journey because with emergence there is always the potential for change and unexpected results from our actions. When we embrace the fluidity of motherhood, and are open to emergence, we can learn to ride the waves of change and breathe into the ongoing shifts, allowing for our positive gifts as mothers to surface.

Reflective questions

What is emerging in you right now?

What has been unexpected on your journey?

Can you embrace new things as they appear and go with the flow, or are you resistant to change?

Activity

Take a blank page and start with the phrase 'My journey as a mother has been . . .' Think about the unexpected things that have emerged on your journey of motherhood. Start writing whatever comes to mind in the moment, don't think or worry about making sense or even making full sentences. Just see what flows out.

MEET THE GODDESS

You are full of energy and power

·

Sense and expand your inner light

·

Connect with your feminine energy

Childbirth, however it happens, connects us with a divine, spiritual, primeval, cosmic energy. We are literally part of the universal energy of creation with our parenting. Our female essence is a mirror of the divine essence of the Goddess. We are full of energy and power. Our maternal wisdom is fed by the maternal wisdom of Earth. Our inner light comes from deep within us, we can sense it and expand it. Gaia is the Earth Goddess, a living, breathing, pulsating being with a higher intelligence. When we meet the Goddess we connect with the pulsating spirituality present on our Mother's Journey.

Practice deep acceptance of not being in charge, there are bigger forces at play with your ongoing Mother's Journey. Paradoxically we are both a tiny insignificant part, and hugely important. Our power echoes the power of the Goddess.

It is humbling to be part of an extensive lineage of women woven from the fabric of creation. Trust in the bigger unfolding picture. There are spiritual, soul connections between you, your child and Gaia. Be rooted in the present moment.

Reflective questions

How do you perceive your feminine way of being?

What were the moments in your life when you felt connected to something that is beyond your human body?

Do you see women around you that are inspiring examples of the embodiment of Goddess energy?

Activity

Take time to connect with Gaia. Feel the power of the elements; the wind, water, rocks and all of life. Connect with yourself and feel the same power moving through your breath, your veins and your bones. Connect with the power of the Goddess within you.

EMPOWER

'Life is not about having a career, or having a lot of money. It is about fulfilling our lives, about being and finding joy in relationships, about giving and receiving . . . It is amazing what can happen to a woman who becomes a mother. She is healing . . . people who are in touch with her may also heal.'

Clara Scropetta, Italian doula

LISTEN

Listen without interruption or judgement

·

Listen to what is beyond words

·

Appreciate the silence

·

Listen to your own body

When we give our full attention to someone and practice deep listening without judgement, we give them the opportunity to follow their own thoughts, ideas and feelings. Interruption-free listening is a big shift from the usual style of conversation where two people are conversing with their own stories, or when the listener brings their own questions and opinions to what is being said. With interruption-free listening, the full attention is on the person talking, no questions are asked and no comments are made. Even if there is silence, the space is held for the person to go deeper and allow other things to surface. This can be a big shift from the cultural norms of conversing and listening, so it is something that we need to consciously practice.

Before our babies can speak we are listening to the way they express themselves and interpret them. As they grow and start to talk, our listening attention may shift from their body language to the words being said. As their capacity to express themselves is still developing let's cultivate our deep listening to grasp what is really happening with them on all levels of being, to catch the information that is beyond words. We can support our children to feel safe and heard by just being present with them and listening rather than speaking, as they express their thoughts and emotions.

Reflective questions

What is your usual inner dialogue when somebody else is speaking?

Are you able to observe and embrace what is being said by others without your own comments and stories coming up?

What is your attitude towards moments of silence that happen in conversations?

In what ways did you notice changes in your ability to truly listen since you became a mother?

Activity

Interruption-free listening and talking time with our partner or friends is a valuable way of connecting with each other and understanding each other's perspective on life. Find a friend, another mother or partner to practice with. Decide on how much time each person will have to speak and who is speaking first. You can answer some of the reflective questions from this guidebook or talk freely about what is happening in your life. While one person is speaking, the other is just deeply listening.

Swap roles when the allocated time is up.

PRACTICE SELF-CARE WITH YOUR CHILD

Nourish yourself while being with your child

·

Have fun with your child

·

Relax and play

·

Take care of yourself TODAY

Mother well-being = baby well-being. And baby well-being = mother well-being. When we understand how interconnected our well-being is with our children's, we no longer need to feel guilty about taking time for self-care. Self-care is fundamental. We need to take responsibility for looking after ourselves, so that we are then able to support our family. Putting time into our own self-care brings us into alignment and personal peace.

One of the big shifts with being a mother is how little time we get on our own, and as we often associate self-care with being alone, we start to long for opportunities for solo time that may never come. A helpful realisation is to find opportunities to practice self-care with our children. Are you nourished by singing, dancing, having a bath, walking, painting, watching birds and clouds? All of these things can be done with our child at any time, instead of wistfully waiting for that golden solo time. When we can integrate caring for ourselves as mothers with our parenting then we have numerous chances. As our child gets older we can swap massages with them.

Self-care comes in many shapes and forms and serves to bring us into greater physical, emotional, mental and spiritual well-being. When we first become mothers our self-care routines might be very much about meeting our basic needs such as washing, eating and drinking enough water and other simple things that we previously took for granted. Now we can be more conscious about them and ensure that they do happen, and celebrate the small successes. As time progresses we can continually redefine what self-care means for us, and how best to nurture ourselves.

Reflective questions

What were the patterns of self-care you had pre-motherhood?

What gives you deep nourishment?

What are your daily and weekly patterns of self-care now?

Activity

Think of an activity that truly nourishes you. Are you used to doing it by yourself? How can you adapt, change and tweak it so that you can do it with your child? Do this activity with your child. Make it a special time, share that they are having special 'mummy time', and that it is going to be an activity that both of you are going to love.

GIVE GRATITUDE

Gratitude is the secret to happiness
·
Gratitude brings presence
·
Being truly grateful is healing

Gratitude predisposes our body and brain to an optimal state of well-being, valuable for our first years of motherhood. Scientific research shows how an attitude of gratitude on a regular basis can upgrade our hormones and our neurotransmitters.[1] If we are thankful for something, we acknowledge that we are happy about it. Therefore, gratitude means cultivating happiness, which is associated with astounding benefits for our health.

Gratitude brings us into presence. When we develop the capacity to pay attention to what's happening in our lives in the present moment, we are present to all the beauty of our world – birdsong, a glint of sunlight on leaves, the sweetness of a sleeping baby.

Gratitude helps us connect to other ways of seeing and feeling, and is a catalyst for generosity, kindness, compassion, and solidarity. Express your gratitude to people in your life – family, friends, and even people in your wider community. Let them know you are grateful for their being and for what they do. Practise this with your child as well. There are many ways we can practise giving gratitude in our everyday life individually as mothers or with our family. We can have a gratitude jar, box or tree at home where we can put small gratitude messages, or we can keep a gratitude journal to draw and write in.

Making gratitude a part of our daily life is a political act.[2] It eases our constant craving for more in our consumer culture and growth economy. Gratitude allows us to discern what we really have, what we really need, and who we really are. We can also choose a practice that is grounded more in our actions, with gestures such as speaking our gratitude, hugging, singing, etc. Gratitude expressed through our creative self, deepens and honours our creative capacity.

Reflective questions

Do you have a regular gratitude practice? Which one is your favourite?

Are you grateful for an experience or situation that was challenging or painful?

Do you express gratitude towards yourself?

Activity

At the end of the day, spend five minutes thinking or writing about 'what went well'. When driving, stuck at the traffic lights, or queuing at the supermarket, count ten things you're grateful for on each of your fingers. It's fast and simple, and it works!

ASK FOR HELP AND BE PROACTIVE

Let your family and community know you need them

Ask for help before things get hopeless

Seek out and nurture friendships

When you are feeling overwhelmed, or juggling with a full plate, ask for help from your 'village'. Call on support from your partner, your family, friends or neighbours. If you don't have the support of your community, reach out to other parents for a babysitting swap, pay for a babysitter, or find a group or club where you can safely leave the children so you can have some time to get things back in order. Help doesn't always come in the form of childcare, though. Help may mean finding someone who can help clean your home, pick up the children from activities or provide a listening ear. Get creative if money is tight and think of ways to ask for help without spending any money – like skill swapping or inviting friends over to help you in return for cooking a dinner for them.

Pay attention to what you're feeling and watch your internal gauge for signs of overwhelm. Don't wait until you are burnt out. Be proactive in asking for help and make sure you take care of your own needs. Losing yourself in motherhood is easy to do when you're working tirelessly to meet the needs of others. However, you cannot fully take care of your children until you take care of yourself.

Motherhood can be lonely when you stay at home every day and get stuck in the same old routine. It is time to be brave and look for opportunities to meet new people and other parents. Do you see another mum walking by herself in your neighbourhood? What would happen if you approached her and said 'hello'? Consider meeting parents through a local mum's group, playgrounds or online meet-up groups for parents.

Reflective questions

Who are the people around you you can rely on?

What does your dream community look like?

What kind of people would you like to meet and have in your life?

What prevents you from reaching out for help?

Activity

Create a give away occasion, it can be face-to-face or online, to invite your friends and family to offer a bit of their time to help each other. The give away can be anything as tangible or intangible. You can set a deadline for the exchange (such as within two weeks or a month), a topic (as cooking, playing with children, tidying up). Be creative to invite your 'village' to create mutual support while having fun.

NOURISH COMMUNITY

Set up a mother's circle

Recognise your allies

Cultivate empathy

Build a support network

During pregnancy, before we even become mothers, we can start to feel the urge to bond with other women. We crave for connection, for a safe place to share and find answers, to be surrounded by peers who can deeply understand what we are experiencing. This can become even stronger after our child is born: we look for experienced mothers to learn from and share with. We are more able to create deep connections with other women and many of us will begin to instinctively build the support network around us that will be key to our well-being in the months and years ahead.

Our capacity to build networks and communities is probably at its best during this age of hyperconnectivity. According to the psychologist Shelley Taylor this is rooted in our evolution.[3] The female response to stress is based on a tend-

and-befriend instinct: when facing danger women would tend to their children and turn to other women for help. Nurturing and building communities, rather than fighting or fleeing.

Higher levels of oxytocin also work as allies for our ability to build communities around us, boosting our empathy and making us able to connect more with our children, and with other mothers. Having a steady community around us allows us to feel more grounded and self-confident, and it is worth devoting some time to building and nurturing it. Finding a community of mothers may enable us to find the strength and ability to make positive changes to our immediate environment, contributing towards building a more family-friendly, nature-connected culture.

Reflective questions

Who are your allies, who can you collaborate with?

How does being part of a community add value to your life?

Which qualities would you love to experience in your community in the coming future?

Activity

Map your network. Draw four concentric circles and fill them in with names or drawings of the people who are part of your network: start from you and your child, the other parent, close family, broader social groups like friends, neighbours, peer mothers. Reflect on what you see.

What works well? What is missing for you? If you could change something, what would you change and what would you create in its place?

TRUST YOUR INTUITION

Ask – what does your intuition say?

Connect with the intuition in your body

Listen and then respond

Your body knows and can guide you

Building trust in yourself is a daily process – building trust in your intuition, your capacities as a mother, trust in your body. The more you tune into your intuition, the more information it can give you about what is right for you and your children in any moment. Just asking the question of yourself – what does my intuition say? – allows you to feel into more possibilities than your intellect alone can give. Trusting your intuition means listening to it and then finding a course of action that resonates with it. Over time you will be able to locate your intuition in particular places in your body and with specific bodily sensations. As you develop your connection with your intuition you are able to rely on its wisdom and respond more fully to it.

Your intuition is also fed by your connection to nature. Building trust in nature and the systems that support life gives us confidence and empowers us to be of service to a bigger picture. Being connected and in harmony with the natural world and its cycles enhances the ability to sense pathways for yourself and your children. Building trust in ourselves allows us to bring our gifts more fully into the world and find our purpose and contribution to the world. The more you come to trust your own intuition the more you can read and respond to your children's intuitive responses, even though they might not understand them as such. The more we are able to trust our intuition, the more we are able to trust and relax into the unfolding journey.

Reflective questions

Where in your body do you feel your intuition is located?

Can you tell a story of a time when you did trust your intuition?

What are the small ways you trust your intuition already e.g. what to wear, eat, when to do certain things?

Activity

Follow your intuition on what you want to eat today. Write down ten different meals on separate bits of paper, add some unhealthy ones and some you don't like. Put the papers upside down so you can't read them, and one by one take a paper and listen to your body's reaction to it. Ask your inner voice to choose the one for you to cook today.

Now either cook this one or another one that speaks to your intuition.

Check in with yourself afterwards how it was to have trusted your intuition.

DESIGN YOUR LIFE PATH

Direct your energies with purpose
·
Grow your effectiveness
·
Follow what is truly important to you
·
Follow your joy

Through design we can assess the direction we want to take and then through action we make steps along the path. Through design we can manifest the life path that we wish to take as a mother. Manifestation might seem like a big fancy notion, but, in our children, we have just manifested a whole human being – there is no end to the possibilities of what we can manifest in our lives and in the world. When we manifest, we bring something into being. On a day to day level, we design all the time, and through that design, we manifest. For example, we think 'I'm hungry', then we design a pathway to manifesting a meal. Designing can be thought of as bringing the process of manifestation to our conscious attention, so that we can direct our energies with purpose and effectiveness. Design can support us to realign our life path as a mother.

For many of us the process of personal transformation that we have been exploring can lead us to examine our direction in life. Becoming a mother can focus our minds on what is truly important to us. We can often find ourselves, as mothers, wanting to positively contribute to the world, to play our part in global healing, to be part of creating a more positive future for all beings, especially our own children. Design can be used to follow our life path on many levels from growing our effectiveness to designing nourishing days for ourselves; from consciously focusing on our relationships to following a business idea.

Reflective questions

What have you manifested in the last week?

What would be your ideal vision of your life path over the next three years? The next ten years?

Where do you see that you were able to manifest something in your past? Can you use the same pattern of behaviour and thinking to manifest something in your life now?

Activity

Design an effective day for yourself. What would be your vision for that day? What are the limits to your effectiveness and the resources you have to support it? Make a plan, do it and then reflect upon how it went.

Next, design a nourishing day for yourself. When you get familiar with designing days for yourself, you can start to design more of your life path.

NOURISH YOUR GIFTS

'Motherhood has given me strength, inspiration, and courage. It's forced me out of my comfort zone more times than I can count and has taught me how to live life in the present . . . I'm stronger than I ever thought possible, I'm patient (well most of the time), I can laugh at myself (because I'll go crazy if I don't) and I have this amazing ability to love unconditionally, as most mothers do.'

Kristin Whiteside, mother and blogger, herviewfromhome.com

FIND YOUR STRENGTH

Trust your inner power
·
Find your balance between steadiness and flexibility
·
Let your courage manifest

Motherhood provides constant training for a new mindset and for many abilities that can be grouped under the word 'strength': energy, flexibility, courage, resilience, endurance, determination, responsibility and hyperdrive.

Riccarda Zezza talks about 'hyperdrive' as the super-energy state triggered by motherhood, that many mothers report.[4] It's about being able to do more things, and better, in the same amount of time. It's about being more effective, focused, goal-oriented, present. You might be close to exhaustion while reading this, but if you take a step back, you will most likely recognise that you actually have learned to channel your energy in a more effective way.

'Responsibility' is the ability to respond to the requests we get from the environment around us. Becoming a mother throws us instantly into a huge world of choices: from pregnancy to birthing, from the first days to the teenage years of our children. Making decisions that involve another person's well-being and thriving (sometimes even survival) becomes a daily task for us. Willing or not, we become bolder and more determined, more effective and self-confident.

Resilience is the ability of a material to absorb a shock without breaking. In psychology, resilience means an individual's ability to adapt in the face of adverse conditions. That's exactly the kind of strength we as mothers are able to develop: a virtuous mix of steadiness and flexibility. We are able to respond in many different ways to unexpected situations and increase our endurance to stress.

Reflective questions

What are your main responsibilities in your life?

What are your strengths?

In what ways are you more resilient since you became a mother?

Activity

Strength isn't always physical, it can come in many forms. Sit down with a bigger piece of paper and some colourful crayons, pencils or watercolours. As you are reflecting on the question of 'What is my strength?'

Let the painting emerge. Place it in a visible space to remind you daily of the power within you.

MOTHERHOOD IS JOY

Recognise beauty around you

·

Nourish your inner child

·

Let yourself bloom

Motherhood can bring with it the ability to see more beauty in the world around us. Just looking at your baby can fill your eyes with tears of awe and joy and fill your heart with love. This is a gift of oxytocin, the 'hormone of love' that fills us during labour and while having skin-to-skin contact with our children.

Having our children around also means being surrounded by loving, wild creatures that are able to love unconditionally, no matter how angry or upset we – or they – may get sometimes. This might be the greatest learning we can get from them. Witness, and be blessed with this capacity of loving unconditionally.

We can experience this ability to feel beauty predominately at the beginning of our Mother's Journey, and may be able to recall those sensations from the early months when we are playing with or lulling our babies, walking in nature, or tasting a specially prepared meal that has been cooked for us. This post-natal bubble of love and beauty that many lucky mothers are surrounded by, is something that can re-shape the way we see the world. It is worth riding the wave and tending this gift of beauty, love and grace, so it doesn't evaporate when time and daily routines come by. A great way to nurture this special sensitivity and receptivity to beauty is by connecting with nature – nature within us and nature outside of us.

Reflective questions

In what kind of places and forms is there beauty around you?

Are you able to see it, and connect with it?

How can you embed more beauty, love and grace in your life?

Activity

Write a love letter. Choose someone or something you want to bless with your love. Your partner, your child, your mother, your house, your community, the nature around you.

Write and tell them why and how you love them, why you are grateful to them. Dare to give, or read them this letter. How does it feel?

YOUR GIFT IS EFFECTIVENESS

Be present
·
Recognise your priorities
·
Acknowledge your superpowers

Once you have a baby to care for, the amount of time at your disposal undergoes a drastic drop. This leads to an unavoidable need to prioritise: you learn to choose, almost without noticing, what is worth doing and what is not, what is worth paying attention to, what can be postponed. You value your time much more, and you are able to fit within the same time frame twice as many things as you could before. The more you proceed on the motherhood pathway, the more it comes naturally.

Having one or more children to take care of also enhances your ability to be able to focus on more than one thing at a time. Think about an evening when you are preparing dinner while your child is playing with a friend in the same room. You know what's going on both on the cooker and with the children. This is what multitasking is all about. We are not able to perform more than one task at once – multi-tasking is a myth, apparently![5] – but we are able to quickly and constantly shift from one task to another, from one focus to another. Motherhood is an effective training ground to hone this skill and mothers can become addicted to this way of existing. Undoubtedly useful as this may be, do not forget to nurture your ability to be fully present.

Reflective questions

What are your superpowers?

Are you able to be fully present when playing with your child, talking to your friends, or cooking a good meal?

Are you aware of your priorities?

Activity

If you are one of those multi-tasking mothers who likes doing two things together while they are thinking about at least five more, try this activity. Find a moment at home when you can devote your time exclusively to your child or your children, and do this exercise for twenty minutes.

Grab a piece of paper and a pencil and just play with your child, doing whatever makes both of you happy. Try to be aware of what comes into your mind. Every time you find your mind wandering away from the activity you are doing, just write down one word about that ('laundry' 'dinner' 'project'), then let go of that thought and focus back on your child, and on what you are doing together. How many times did you find your mind wandering?

EMBRACE YOUR VULNER-ABILITY

Accept the unknown

Being vulnerable makes you stronger

Shed your armour and show your real self

The ability to be vulnerable opens unexpected doors

Feeling vulnerable may sometimes be hard to cope with. Having lots of open questions, doubts or insecurities is not a comfortable feeling. On the other hand, the ability to be vulnerable includes the ability to not be at our best – and to show it. To be able to ask for help, to be able to accept that we make mistakes. To be able to say: 'Today, I cannot do it'. That's very much part of being a human. As mothers we often think about ourselves as super-beings, the ones that can never fail, never show fatigue. Remember that no matter what you think or how you have been raised, we are all entitled to be tired, vulnerable or overwhelmed.

We invite you to learn how to embrace vulnerability as part of your human nature and reframe it as an ability and a strength. We need to learn how to show vulnerability, how to communicate it gently and to accept it, to ask for help and to learn how to delegate tasks. Showing vulnerability, rather than being seen as a weakness, could open unexpected doors. When you are able to show that you are vulnerable, people around you will be called to be more empathetic, understanding and open. After all, isn't it much easier and pleasant to empathise with friends when they open their heart to you about their insecurities, rather than when they appear to perform perfectly, never missing a shot?

Reflective questions

How do you feel when you show your vulnerability? What emotions emerge?

What stops you from being vulnerable?

What doors would open for you, if you allowed yourself to be vulnerable?

Activity

Next time you find yourself facing the unknown – uncontrollable tears, unexpected illness, unpredicted rush of anger – stop for a moment to listen to yourself. How does it feel? What are your impulses?

What is your pattern of behaviour at times like this? Do you reach out to your smartphone to ask Google? Do you feel frustrated? Angry? A victim?

Can you embrace the sensation of not being in control?

BECOME SELF-AWARE

Observe your patterns

Discover your true nature

Acknowledge your roots

A Mother's Journey can be a journey through self-awareness. Our children enable us to develop a habit of self-awareness: awareness of our emotions, trigger points, limits, patterns and strengths. When it comes to relationships with friends and partners, we can generally decide to finish the relationship and move on, if conflicts become too demanding. With our children this is not possible, and the only solution to conflicts and hardships is to face them, observe our patterns, accept them and resolve them. The process of becoming more self-aware might not always be pleasant, but in the long run, it is part of the never-ending journey of self-development.

Motherhood can be a great opportunity to reshape the relationship with our family, parents and ancestors; to understand our roots. This is a great moment to build or re-build a connection with the female line in your family.

You can do this by talking to your mother, aunts and grandmothers, to harvest the feminine wisdom, stories and wounds your ancestors have carried; to learn about their ways of tending their children, their health remedies, their cooking secrets, their stories and more.

Becoming a parent can also facilitate a reconciliation with our father, observing him as a grandfather and interacting with him from a different role and a new identity in the family. The birth of a new human being is a powerful moment for the entire family to recalibrate – take this opportunity to participate in re-shaping your family patterns.

Reflective questions

Which are the strongest 'buttons' that your children are pressing?

Which patterns of your behaviour are they asking you to confront?

What behaviour or pattern of thinking can you be proud to say that you have changed?

What was your biggest 'a-ha moment' or realisation you have had about yourself in the last three months?

Activity

Practice gratitude towards your mother: no matter what the relationship with your mother is, list ten things you are grateful for in her. If you are brave enough, find a way to share it with her!

RECEIVE THE GIFT OF PATIENCE

Motherhood is training in emotional intelligence

·

Patience is a gift to use and practice

·

Cultivate patience through resting

Emotional intelligence is 'the ability to monitor one's own and others' feelings, to discriminate among them, and to use this information to guide one's thinking and action'.[6] Based on empathy, love and compassion, emotional intelligence is a set of skills that can be developed. As mothers, we are unconsciously doing this most of the time.

'When it concerns our children, there is no task, there is no communication that does not involve both mind and heart'.[7] Spending a fair amount of one-on-one time with a child provides daily training for our emotional intelligence. As children are mostly driven by emotion and in the early years unable even to communicate with words, we have to be more attentive and open to unspoken language, to listening, to deeply understanding their mood and inner world.

Emotional intelligence and opening us to a deeper, heartfelt understanding of other beings, is also a catalyst for patience. The word patience comes from the Latin word *pati* and the Greek word πάσχειν (paskein): to feel, to receive a sensation, to endure without reacting. Perhaps one of the most difficult spiritual attributes to possess! It is not always easy to be patient with ourselves, with our children or with others. Often patience comes wrapped in trials and hardships, but it can be seen as a gift to unwrap and use. Of course, when we are well-rested, healthy and feeling happy with our life in general we are more able to be patient.

Reflective questions

Which situation in life is currently testing your patience?

When looking back, which are the situations in which patience helped you face frustration or adversity?

How can you cultivate patience with your children?

Activity

When you realise you are getting impatient STOP and try this mindfulness exercise in which each letter stands for a step.

S is for stop what you are doing, such as rushing, nagging or reacting.
T is for take three breaths. This will anchor and help you to slow down.
O is for observe what you are feeling, notice how your body is reacting and ask yourself 'why am I losing my patience right now?'
P is for proceed, continuing the task that needs to be done.

EMBRACE YOUR FEMININE POWER

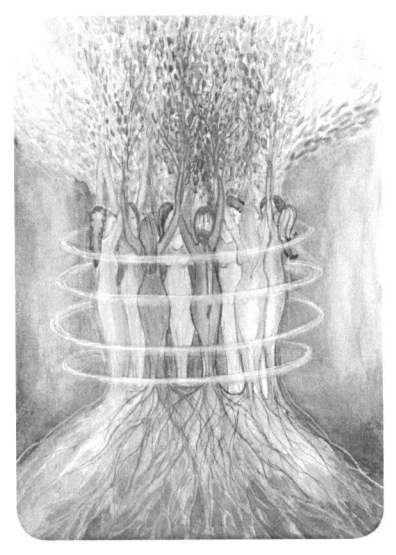

Discover and celebrate your cycles

·

Follow the Moon cycle

·

Spend time in nature

·

Allow yourself to do nothing

Reconnecting with our bodies during pregnancy and birth is a powerful way to realise what it means to live in a female body. As we re-adjust our lives to our new role, we learn to allow things to happen instead of trying to control them. During pregnancy and birth we experience needing to let things happen in their natural rhythm. Taking care of our well-being and 'me time' is valuable for ourselves and for our children. Doing nothing is not a sign of laziness, it is an important part of taking care of ourselves. Every hour of recharging will benefit our children. Maureen Murdock, in her book *The Heroine's Journey*, states 'Finding out about being instead of doing is the sacred task of the Feminine . . . And our planet, Gaia needs this wisdom, of mindful being to get into a right relationship with all living beings.'[8]

In ancient India, the mantra of Adi Shakti was devoted to the Divine Mother that encompasses the creative energy living in each of us. Ancient Indian wisdom calls women the First Teachers and states that the power of the mother's prayer is the strongest force in the Universe. To support ourselves in our full grace, we need female company. Women circles hold the power of listening. We all need a place where we feel unconditionally accepted and listened to with deep attention and no judgement, where we can be our fullest selves. Mother Earth can provide you with the same quality, and can surround you and sustain you with the healing energy of plants and other forms of life.

Reflective questions

In what ways are natural cycles present in your day to day life?

When was the last time you consciously spent time doing nothing?

What are the feminine aspects you appreciate in yourself the most?

Activity

Being rather than doing is the ultimate feminine quality. We invite you to practice this skill in nature, which is the most feminine part of Creation. Organise a day or half day of childcare if possible. Get out alone to a site of natural beauty, a place that speaks to you. If you need to take a car or bus trip, allow yourself the time for it. If your baby is still breastfeeding, take someone with you who can be with your child. With someone lovingly taking care of your child, you may have at least two hours of relaxed free time, especially if you pick your child's nap time. Take a journal, some drinks and food, and nothing else. Switch off your mobile phone. Get yourself out there, stop talking, open your senses. Do nothing else, just BE surrounded by Life. Allow yourself at least two hours of free, unstructured time in nature.

CONNECT WITH NATURE

'See how nature – trees, flowers, grass- grows in silence; see the stars, the moon and the sun, how they move in silence . . . We need silence to be able to touch souls.'

Mother Teresa

GET OUT, GET WILD!

Reconnect with nature

It's time to let nature fully into your life

Nature is everywhere

For thousands and thousands of years nature has been our natural habitat: the light of the day, the cool of the night, the flow of the seasons, the sensation of the sun, rain, and wind. A deep bond with nature is embedded in our genes affecting our mind and body. But somehow along the way we seem to have forgotten it. Slowly but surely we left nature behind and we went inside, replacing nature with ceilings and walls, central heating and artificial light. Today some of us spend 90 per cent of our lives indoors and we are passing this new habit onto our children. Based on the statistics, the coming generations will be indoors from the moment they wake up and throughout most of the day, spending most of their time in closed off environments. Living without daylight and fresh air can strongly affect our health and wellbeing.

How can we find ways to let nature back into our lives? Our lungs, body and mind are longing for it. To nurture and value the connection with Mother Nature we need to get up, get out and get wild! Nature is all around us; it can be woodland, a community garden, a park, a farm or the nursery or school grounds. Even a very small outdoor space can be a rich resource if we create the opportunities for creative play. Being and playing outside with our children is exciting, motivating and fascinating.

The more we play the more we laugh. By experiencing time in nature we feel part of it and we form a connection which is deep, rooted and necessary.

Reflective questions

What are your past experiences of connecting with nature – with plants, animals, water, fire, stones etc.?

Can you remember the last time you had fun in nature alone or with your children?

- *Can you recall the feeling of walking barefoot, touching a tree, petting a cat, looking up at the stars while laying down on the ground?*

Activity

Take a walk on a regular basis instead of driving or getting the bus.

Enjoy daylight, breath fresh air, stretch your legs, play with your children and take in the plants, the weather, the surroundings.

YOU ARE NATURE

Engage all your senses
·
All of nature mirrors you
·
Connect with the fundamental cycle of living and dying
·
Open your heart to interconnectedness

As women we are inevitably tied into the cycles that define all life. They pulse through us and thereby allow us to connect with this pulse of life in the most obvious and experiential way. We experience qualities of life in our bodies and minds, which reflect the same qualities that can be found in the more-than-human world. Through our menstrual cycle we are deeply, intrinsically tied into the fundamental cycle of living and dying. Whereas pregnancy allows us to experience an essential principle of life: interconnectedness. When giving birth we also experience the full force of life. We experience the incomprehensible phenomenon of creating and birthing life through our own bodies. It is a beautiful miracle that we get to embody, which gives us every reason to celebrate it. It is part of our nature and part of the power that we hold.

We know everything is connected to everything else. All life forms are interconnected. All of nature mirrors us and we mirror all of nature. As well as being mirrored through the relationships we have with other human beings, we are mirrored through the more-than-human world. To truly incorporate all of nature as part of us we need to practice and remember. We need to take time to really see the living world surrounding us, to perceive it with all our senses and to recognise its meaning. This living world tells us something about ourselves. Outer nature can be a strong mirror for our inner nature because ultimately, we are One.

Reflective questions

How would you define 'nature'?

Are humans and human-made environments part of your definition of nature?

When do you most feel the interconnectedness of all of life?

Activity

Find an outdoor space and let your attention be drawn to another living being (e.g. animal, plant). Fully enter that other beings' world. Ask yourself the following questions:

Which feature of this being is my attention drawn to?
What does this being feel like to me (do I feel love, sadness, kinship)?
What does it tell me?
What connects us?
How is this being like me? How am I like this being?

YOUR CHILD IS YOUR NATURE MENTOR

Let your child lead the way

·

Be curious

·

Slow down

·

Open yourself to awe and wonder

There is a beautiful and simple truth that is very liberating once we fully let it sink in: every time we spend time outdoors with our children we not only cultivate their connection with the more-than-human world but also our own. In this way your own child is your personal portal to the more-than-human world.

Children are often like little microscopes (on two feet) with highly sensitive antennas. They spot things and perceive a level of detail that we, as adults, often overlook.

In nature this is an eye-opener and uncovers worlds if not universes: children can be mesmerised by tracking a little ant carrying a huge bread crumb, or they notice how a tree sheds its bark. And the admirable thing is that they not only notice but they wonder about these things. They ask, Why are they doing it? Does the tree freeze now? Why is the ant not eating the crumb immediately? This is the gift that we can rediscover through our children. Yes, we theoretically know about the amazing abilities of ants but can we let ourselves be carried away by this? If you slow down, and let your child lead the way you can reconnect with and strengthen your curiosity and sense of awe and wonder. Allow your child to take you on a journey of discovery.

Besides this, there are many scientifically supported benefits that your child can naturally gain along the way. For example, spending time in nature can facilitate a secure attachment between you and your child and it also reduces children's stress, increases curiosity and creativity, improves physical coordination and reduces attention deficit disorder (ADD) symptoms.[9]

Reflective questions

What can your child teach you and what could you teach your child about nature?

What was it like for you to be in nature as a child?

What holds you back from spending time outside in nature? What happens if you do it anyway?

Activity

Go outside and turn your attention to the plants and animals around you. You can pick a tree that stands out to you or a little bug at your feet. With your child, start to imagine and create stories around the lives of these beings as you imagine them. Give them names, let your imagination run free.

CARE FOR EARTH

Be compassionate to all living beings
·
Your everyday actions make a difference
·
Become a role model for your child
·
Honour future generations

Our decisions and actions are having an immeasurable impact upon the environment and our future generations. Native American tribal leaders used the guidance of the Children's Fire: before making any important decisions they asked the question 'Is this decision honouring the life of children to come and all life forms?'

To care for Earth means to apply the following permaculture ethics in our decisions and actions: Earth Care – Does it support the Earth's living eco-systems? People care – Does it have a positive impact on the wellbeing of all people involved or affected by it? Fair Share – Does it take into account the setting of fair limits and the re-distribution of surplus?

Care for Earth is about working in harmony with nature in order to minimise negative impact and maximise positive impact upon our planet. We may carefully reassess the material goods we need and choose products that minimise environmental impact.

As mothers we become even more sensitive and mindful about caring for life. We can become role models for our children of how to appreciate, love and protect the Earth, by cultivating and promoting compassionate concern for our natural world, empathy for our fellow creatures, and a sense of wonder and fascination.

Reflective questions

How can you support your children in establishing a life-long love relationship with the web of Life?

Consider how each of your daily actions will affect the life of your great-great grandchildren?

How is care for Earth present in the choice of goods you purchase and services you use?

What kind of world do you want to create for your children?

Activity

Take an inventory in your home: look at your clothes, your children's clothes, cleaning and sanitary products, food items. Investigate alternative products that minimise harm, waste and use of natural resources. Make your next shopping list based on the alternative products.

Activity

Imagine seven generations into the future. Write a letter, poem or make a piece of art from or to one of your future descendants. Depict a world where every decision made honours future generations and all living beings.

GROUND YOURSELF

Find quick paths to personal peace
·
Connect with earth, air, water and fire
·
Mother with peace and presence

Staying grounded as a mother supports us to take care of ourselves and our families with peace and presence. Everyday challenges can throw us off balance and we need ways to bring ourselves back into alignment. As mothers it is useful to have some quick fixes to ground us and bring us into a state of peace. We can look to the elements of nature; earth, air, water and fire, for inspiration on how to ground ourselves. For earth we can imagine roots coming out of our feet, extending deep into the soil, anchoring and stabilising us, doing this outside and barefoot is even more effective. A simple glass of water refreshes and rehydrates us, reminding us to be fluid and flow with life. Lighting a candle calms our spirit and reminds us of the mystery and luminescence of life. Deep breaths connect us with ourselves and the rhythm of life. We can imagine all our worries leaving with the exhale and being refilled with love, patience and energy on the inhale. Just simply stepping outside can connect us with the elements and bring us into our body. Each of these elements can help us connect with ourselves, and the bigger natural support systems around us. These instant solutions can be combined with our regular self-care practices to give us a framework for being connected and peaceful.

Reflective questions

Which of the four elements, earth, air, water and fire, would be helpful to you right now?

What is your personal practice of bringing yourself into the present moment?

Activity

Step outside, if you can, sit on the ground or stand barefoot. Feel the air on your face, take deep breaths into your belly. Is the fire element present with the sun, or is the water element present with rain or perhaps both or neither is present? Feel the earth you are sitting on and imagine you have roots extending deep into the ground, intertwining with other plant and tree roots. Your roots bring you stability and strength. Imagine those roots extending all the way into the fiery centre of the planet. Imagine your roots drawing up all the energy and support you need. When you feel ready to move, imagine your roots moving with you, still supporting you.

CONNECT WITH THE PLANT WORLD

Grow plants with your child

·

Connect with the plants around you

·

Watch something grow

·

Open yourself to the healing power of plant medicine

Connecting to the natural world in wild places comes easily to us most of the time. However, even in our everyday lives there is a whole world of plants that are constantly accompanying us in one way or the other. We just need to sharpen our awareness for them.

You can cultivate a new habit of regularly noticing the trees and plant life in your daily life, the plants at home, the herbs you cook with, the natural scents you may have in your skin products, the smell of blooming trees and flowers and the natural remedies that you may already use for health and well-being.

As long as you do it consciously, anything from gardening to cooking, to drinking herbal tea can help you to connect with the plant world. Plants have a lot to offer. They can help you meet your physical and psychological needs. Naturally, during pregnancy and breast feeding, we are led back to this world either by choice, or because some allopathic medicines are contraindicated. Pregnancy can be a time when we (re-)open the door to the healing power of natural remedies and our connection with them. This period invites us to connect with the plants, at a time when our intuition is sharpening and we are being asked to tune in more deeply to what our body needs. In contrast to the quick-fix culture, the relationship we have with the plants is cyclical, seasonal, it shows us a slower, more gentle pace. Connecting with and using plant medicine during pregnancy, and with our children is an opportunity for deep connection with self, and the more-than-human world. It is a gift.

Take your child along on this journey by cultivating curiosity for the plants; explore the smell, the shape and (when edible), the taste. Consider planting seeds together, let your child experience what it means to grow something.

Reflective questions

How does the smell of lavender make you feel like? How about the smell of a rose?

How well do you know the character of your plants at home?

Do you know which plants are growing in your neighbourhood?

Activity

With your child go and collect herbs, wild 'weeds' and flowers out in the wild or an urban garden. Study the plants, smell them and look them up online and in books. Make sure they are edible. Go home and cook something with your edible herbs and try to be as conscious as possible while smelling, preparing and eating them. Notice how they taste, what they remind you of and how they make you feel. Give gratitude to the spirit of the plant that you are able to experience so intensely in this moment.

ALIGN WITH NATURAL PATTERNS AND CYCLES

You are winter, spring, summer and autumn

Celebrate the diversity within you

Follow the pattern of waxing and waning

Be mindful of your needs

If you look at nature as a whole there is a cyclical and never-ending pattern of waxing and waning. You can find it anywhere in nature because it is the ultimate principle of life itself and therefore part of human nature. We are born, we grow and eventually, we die.

This magical cycle is especially present in women with our capacity to give life and through our monthly menstrual cycle that we experience for many years of our lives.

Sadly, our current culture is dominated by masculine principles like progress, efficiency and a general maxim of pushing through and being active. This makes it immensely difficult to be in sync with our natural female cycle, especially in the second half of our menstrual cycle.

In this luteal phase, our hormonal system actually asks us to decelerate. Our performance is not as high as we are used to and we process our emotions differently.

Being tied into the cycles that define all life is a challenge and a gift in times like these. It can be a challenge because it contradicts the common lifestyle and our personal idea of what it means to be 'performing well'. It is a gift because it is a gateway that connects us to who we truly are: striving, strong, alert and vibrant and also introspective, vulnerable, brooding and dreaming. We are the full cycle: winter, spring, summer and autumn – every month!

Our bodies can actually guide us to harmonise with this omnipresent cycle pattern of waxing and waning. And if we sincerely listen to this cycle we may start to experience the diversity of our full being.

This is especially important for us mothers as we are constantly confronted with numerous demands and needs- often simultaneously. This can easily make us slip into a 'hamster in a wheel' mode.

We tend to forget that being constantly active and ticking off the lists does not necessarily lead to the moments of stillness, space for introspection and the peace of mind we long for.

We need to consciously create those spaces in our lives in order to bring our full diversity of being to life.

Reflective questions

How aware are you of your female cycle and associated needs?

Do you allow yourself to enter both active and passive ways of being?

What are your personal benchmarks for 'how well' you are doing in your life that you have consciously or subconsciously adopted?

Activity

With the help of your calendar track your menstrual cycle. Once you have tracked the second phase of your cycle, resolve NOT to do one thing that you think you should do but actually feels inappropriate now.

Slowly extend this practice by dissolving more and more 'shoulds' until you feel that you truly have your own permission to live differently, especially during that phase of your cycle.

MOTHER NATURE CIRCLES GUIDE

Mother Nature circles are easy to set up. Essentially it is a gathering of women ready to share and listen to each other. All you need is a set of Mother Nature cards, a space to meet and a few friends. The easiest way to run them is to ask mothers to choose one card that resonates with where they currently are with their Mother's Journey. They can then share with each other in pairs about why they choose this card. After this round you can ask them to choose a second card (having put the first cards back) for the wisdom of their heart that they wish to carry forward. Then ask them to share their thoughts with the whole circle.

The cards and images contain the wisdom needed to support the group to share deeply with each other, so it really is simple for you to run a Mother Nature circle with no specific training. Below is more detail about how to run the circle. Give it a try and see what happens. You can then ask the women when they would like to meet again.

ABOUT MOTHER NATURE CIRCLES

The main intention is that women meet as equals in conversation to share their experiences and to learn together and from each other. Therefore a professional is not needed to lead the circle. Mother Nature circles are different from our Mother Nature Journey Courses, led by trained facilitators. You can find out more about the courses on our Facebook page and website.

Each circle is different as it is emerging from the women that meet and their available resources, such as time, space and interest. Therefore each circle will decide for themselves:

Where you meet: circles can take place in a living room, cafe or a yoga studio. Perhaps you meet each time in a different place or always at the same place.

When you meet: the group can meet once a week or once a month. At a time that suits the group, which may be different from meeting to meeting. The meeting can take place for one hour or one day and everything in between.

What you do: in the coming part of this chapter we propose a loose structure of how to start and finish the circle meeting and what the possible content could be.

Whether babies and children can be present? For mothers who participate, this is part of our 'me time', so the best option is to find someone to look after your children while you are at the meetings although this can be a challenge to find childcare and children can integrate well if they are provided with an appropriate space and activity. Be aware of how this may affect the dynamic of the circle, and each person's ability to feel safe to share.

FLOW OF THE CIRCLE MEETINGS

Decide on the topic of the meeting in advance or on the spot. The topic of the circle meeting is up to you and you can follow your needs around the topics you choose to discuss or you can use the Mother Nature Card Deck and Guidebook. Perhaps each meeting one person draws a card which will become the topic of the meeting. You can then read about it in the guidebook, and share the proposed activity with the group. You can answer the reflective questions in pairs using the deep listening guidelines below.

Circle

We are inviting you to create a setting which is relaxed, enjoyable and gives people a sense of community. We encourage you to literally sit in a circle if possible. The circle is an ancient approach for people to gather, as it gives the opportunity for us all to see each other as we speak. Sometimes it is too intense or distracting to look at people directly and you can decide to put some meaningful objects in the middle, where you can rest your eyes while speaking or listening. In the middle you can place a scarf with some flowers in a pot or light a candle or whatever makes sense to you to create a symbolic 'centre'. You can also use the cards as a central mandala.

Establish group agreements at the first gathering

Confidentiality is an important one. Anything that has been said in the circle remains in the circle, not to be mentioned elsewhere, and not to be mentioned in front of each other during informal times. The right to pass and not share or participate in an activity is also an important agreement to have. Ask the group for any other ground rules, that makes them feel comfortable and safe.

Starting the meetings

Starting with a simple one minute silence brings us into the heart space, grounds us and can be a nice start for each meeting to leave aside the many things that are happening in our lives, and be present.

Announcements

Announcements are an opportunity to mention how long the meeting will be, where the toilets are, when the next meeting will be, and any other logistics or information people want to share.

Sharing circle

Sharing circles are invitations to all the participants to speak to the circle by sharing something. We can do this by passing around a talking piece (eg. a stone, talking stick, toy, ball . . .) and whoever has the talking piece has the attention of the whole group. Each time the talking piece is passed around the circle, you can introduce a question or a theme, and people are invited to respond when the talking piece comes to them. You may like to make the first round a simple name and stating something you are grateful for, before the circle begins to move into deeper topics. If the group is meeting again the first round can be 'Is there an experience you would like to share with the group that has happened since we last met?'

Sometimes people don't feel like sharing something and that is perfectly OK. We welcome their silence and as they pass the talking piece the sharing circle continues. Those who don't have the talking piece are invited to practice deep listening, which means that their hearts are open and they try not to judge what others are saying and don't interrupt with questions or comments.

Mother Nature Card Deck

Mothers can each pick one of the Mother Nature Cards in response to the question 'How do you feel right now?'. Instead of this, or as a second round you can pick one or more cards in response to the question 'What is the wisdom of the heart that I need to take forward?' This will give you inspiration and guidance for the coming days and weeks. The cards can be laid out with the images facing up, or they can be placed the other way up, overlapping so that only the Mother Nature logo is showing, or with all or some of the text showing. Each of these ways invite women to connect with their intuition on different levels, for the wisdom they need in the moment.

Timekeeping

Timekeeping is important for the meeting. With the sharing rounds, it might be appropriate to give people a timeframe for how long they have to speak, so that everyone gets the same amount of time, and it allows the meeting to finish on time. Use a chime and a watch to monitor, or pass the watch and let people monitor the time for the person before them, and pass the watch on when they have finished. With small groups or less time pressure this might not be appropriate.

Deep listening

Deep listening in pairs allows insights to surface and makes time together truly nurturing and special. It also helps us to reconnect with ourselves and really feel heard and acknowledged by others.

You can do this exercise either by following the reflective questions for each principle in this guidebook or from questions or topics that arise from the group. Create pairs by either inviting people to turn to their neighbour or ask them to get up and randomly mix to find a person they don't know that well. Once in pairs, introduce the guidelines of listening pairs as follows:

> *'One person will answer to the question, the other listens, keeps silence and supports the speaker with her full attention. This is an unusual form of communication: there is no dialogue, one person speaks, the other only listens and does not comment or ask questions. If any question or comment arises: the listener can park them internally. We connect with the speaker through our full attentive body language. The question is . . .'*

Decide how much time is given for the first person to speak and make sure that the other person in the pair has the same amount of time available. Two to five minutes per question is usually a good amount of time for this. After each person has shared you can give some more time to share freely with your pair or with the whole group how they felt about the experience.

Options for what to do before the closing round

Journalling and giving some time for the women in the group to take out their notebooks and write down their insights, emotions they feel or ideas that emerged.

Music to release and let go. This activity depends on what the space allows. Select one to three songs that would fit, they can be either meditative, inviting people to lay down or more dynamic, inviting people to dance. Play the music and invite people to be guided by it into stillness or movement.

Three messages is about sharing our collective intelligence and trusting our intuition. Start by giving each participant three small empty pieces of paper (approximate size 8 x 5cm). You can play music in the background and give them a few minutes to write one statement on each piece of paper about what they are taking home from the meeting. Collect all the papers, mix them and make three rounds of the circle, where each person randomly chooses one message to share with the group on each round.

Closing round is an opportunity to consolidate and conclude the circle. Pass the talking piece one last time and invite people to share their feelings, what they've learnt, or perhaps a simple round of gratitude if time is limited.

Thank you for reading the Mother Nature Guidebook. We would like to stay in touch and connect with you. Find out more about our retreats, courses and events on our Facebook page.

ABOUT THE AUTHORS

Ági Berecz

Agi has been working in environmental education since 2004, she has mainly worked in the fields of youth work and adult learning for sustainability. Being inspired by ecopsychology, deep ecology and the path of yoga her interest has been shifting to the inner dimensions of personal transformation. She is founder of Pandora Egyesület in Hungary. She lives in a village in Hungary, coordinates the international 'Mother Nature' project and above all she is a mother of two young girls. Within the project she is mainly dedicated to calling together strong support groups for mothers.

Valentina Cifarelli

Valentina, dynamic doer and passionate visionary. In 2005 she started her journey designing, managing and facilitating international projects for young adults. Since then, she has been researching and developing ways to support and guide people 'in transition' to become aware of their talents and potentials, enabling them to take part authentically and freely in a world rich of challenges and opportunities. When coaching and empowering people she loves to use non formal education for mutual and dynamic learning and permaculture to grow social, environmental and economic resilience. After working in the private and public sector, Valentina in 2014 co-founded Paradiso Ritrovato and with this step became captain of her own adventure. She is a mother, living with her precious family in a little community in the hills of Romagna, in Italy. Here she takes care of bees, plants and people experiencing the enriching and challenging life of an intentional community with other people.

Sara Galeotti

Sara is a facilitator, a graphic designer and a graphic facilitator. She has been designing Mother Nature visual identity with love and care. She works and lives at Casa del cuculo, a community of three families based on the lovely hills of Emilia Romagna in Italy. As a facilitator and a trainer, she is engaged in different projects related to community development, capacity building and vocational education. She loves travelling, baking vegan desserts, and drawing with her daughter. She is mother of Greta and Livio and was waiting for her second child while writing and designing this book.

Lara Kastelic

Lara is curious and passionate about sustainable lifestyles that brings together ecological and social aspects. After completing her studies of Biology she spent a year in an ecovillage in Germany, immersing herself into a way of living based on the values of Earth Care and People Care. In 2014 Lara returned to Slovenia and has since been engaged in several permaculture and alternative education projects. She currently works with children, youth and adults. She joined this project as she felt this will be an amazing learning journey that can support her in her own relationship with motherhood.

Jana Lemke

Jana is an author, a professionally trained Zen Yoga teacher, psychologist and systemic therapist in training with an emphasis on mindfulness approaches. She is also a curious mother. Because of that (but not only!) her passion lies in working with women in times of transition, particularly mothers. Jana is a trained process facilitator in wild nature and has facilitated and accompanied several programmes for young adults, which included twenty-four-hour solos in the wild as well as a three-day solo, the so-called vision quest in the wilderness. Based on her personal experience she decided to research and write a PhD about this nature-based practice. In 2018 it was published as a book (*Exploring Human Nature: A Reflexive Mixed Methods Enquiry into Solo Time in the Wilderness*). For Jana, the Mother Nature Project is an exciting and unique opportunity to weave together those strands she personally and professionally feels very deeply about: working with women, rites of passage, process work, creativity and the more-than-human world.

Looby Macnamara

Looby is a mother of two wonderful daughters, one already grown up, and the other growing up fast. She is author of *People and Permaculture*, *7 Ways to Think Differently* and *Strands of Infinity*. *People and Permaculture* is the first book globally to translate the use of permaculture principles and design for people based systems. She is the creator of the Design Web, a holistic design framework that has been used thousands of times globally for all sorts of personal and social designs. She has been chair of the Permaculture Association Britain and is a senior diploma tutor. She lives on a twenty-acre smallholding in Herefordshire, where she runs an education and demonstration centre – Applewood Permaculture Centre. Looby is co-founder of the Cultural Emergence project to support personal and global shifts towards a regenerative culture. She is researching and developing Cultural Emergence as a profoundly effective toolkit to be shared in her forthcoming book. www.LoobyMacnamara.com

ORGANISATIONS

Pandora Association

Pandora Association was founded in 2012 and is based in Budapest, Hungary. Its aim is to transmit knowledge and practical alternatives within the fields of living in harmony with nature, active citizenship and community building for a sustainable world by promoting the worldview and philosophy as well as applying the methodology of deep ecology. Pandora disseminates the approach of deep ecology, voluntary simplicity and permaculture. It creates time and space for collective learning and experience, and develops a global vision that promotes conscious and harmonious co-existence with nature. Learning is a holistic process that takes the trinity of body, mind and soul into account, it respects and pays attention to all the participants and the community. Pandora is the leading organisation of the Mother Nature strategic partnership.

www.en.pandora.org.hu

Paradiso Ritrovato

Paradiso Ritrovato (Regained Paradise) is a non profit organisation, based in Italy and founded in 2012 by four women that have been studying and researching for years in Italy and abroad on the theme of sustainability within education. Our mission is to spread knowledge and practical alternatives in two main fields which are education for sustainability and finding vocation.

www.paradisoritrovato.org

Preplet

Ecological, Social and Cultural Association for Creative Community, is a NGO from the town Grosuplje in Slovenia. A group of women from the local environment have been working together since 2007 with the general objective of establishing opportunities for children and youth to find their own creative expression. Our work is based on the values of ecological sustainability and social inclusion. We engage with young people to organise activities for children in local area. Our activities are also aimed at Roma children and we are collaborating with young Roma people.

www.preplet.org

Casa del cuculo

Casa del cuculo is a cooperative based in Emilia-Romagna, Italy, founded in 2010 by four people who have been researching and experimenting together on the themes of community building and social research through non-formal methods. Casa del cuculo's mission is to tailor-work cultural projects, products and processes aimed at producing social and cultural innovation and urban regeneration through the following methodologies: visual, performing and public arts, facilitation, community building, research, graphic design and data visualisation, advising and training.

www.casadelcuculo.org

Permaculture Association UK

The Permaculture Association supports and empowers people to design thriving communities by applying permaculture ethics and principles. As well as being based in the UK, the Association contributes to permaculture worldwide. It has a participatory structure so members can be directly involved. The Association aims to nurture, grow and enhance collaboration within permaculture and related networks. Using permaculture design empowers people to make informed choices towards a sustainable, regenerative future. By putting ethics first and using natural systems as a guide, there are simple and innovative ways to live fairly and regeneratively now and in the future.

www.permaculture.org.uk

Camino E.V.

Camino e.V. is a member of the society for Educational Aids and since 2006 a state-approved carrier of the youth welfare service organisation. In 2006, the association was founded and took over tasks in the context of public youth welfare, for example the accompaniment and support of children, young people and families in conflicts and problematic life situations. The motivation of the founding members is to 'build bridges' to make new goals attainable for young people.

www.camino-team.de

Mural Moral – Color Space Association

The Colour-Space Association of Pécs was created through the cooperation of youth workers and professionals on community development, with the aim to empower disadvantaged groups of young people, to promote voluntary work and improve the national and international professional cooperation. The association has experience with different kinds of women groups, specialising in working with women living with difficulties: strengthening young women prisoners with community arts or community building activities in Pécsbánya, Pécs. The goal is served by community arts (mural painting, theatre, movement, music, media, other visual techniques) and non-formal educational methods, trainings, and spreading materials about our work.

www.muralmoral.org

ENDNOTES

[1] Emmons, R. A. (2003). 'Personal Goals, Life Meaning, and Virtue: Wellsprings of a Positive Life' in C. L. M. Keyes & J. Haidt (Eds.), *Flourishing: Positive Psychology and the Life Well-lived* (pp. 105–128). Washington, DC, US: American Psychological Association.

[2] Macy J. and Johnstone C. (2011). *Active Hope: How to Face the Mess We're in Without Going Crazy.* New World Library.

[3] Taylor, S.E. (2002). *The Tending Instinct: How Nurturing is Essential to Who We Are and How We Live.* New York: Holt

[4] Zezza R. Vitullo A. (2014) *Maam – La maternità è un master.* Milano: Bur

[5] Rock, D. (2009) *Your Brain at Work: Strategies for Overcoming Distraction, Regaining Focus, and Working Smarter All Day Long.* New York: HarperBusiness

[6] Salovey P. Grewal D. (2005) 'The Science of emotional intelligence', in *Current Direction in Phycological Science.* Yale University. http://www.cogsci.rpi.edu/files/5065

[7] Zezza R. Vitullo A. (2014) *Maam – La maternità è un master.* Milano: Bur

[8] Murdock M. (1990) *The Heroine's Journey.* Boulder, Colorado: Shambhala

[9] St. Antoine, S., Charles, C., & Louv, R. (2013). *Together in Nature: Pathways to a Stronger, Closer Family*. Minneapolis, MN: Children and Nature Network. Retrieved from https://www.childrenandnature.org/wp-content/uploads/2015/08/FamilyBonding_En_20141.pdf.

Other resources

Campbell, J. (1949) *The Hero with a Thousand Faces*, Pantheon Books, New York

Macnamara, L. (2012) *People and Permaculture; Designing Personal, Collective and Planetary Well-being*, Permanent Publications, Hampshire, UK.

Thich Nhat Hanh (2010) *Reconciliation: Healing the Inner Child*, Parallax Press, Berkeley, California.